HU-6770

P9-DOF-500

# What Manner of Man?

# WHAT MANNER
# OF MAN?

Noel F. Busch

HARPER & BROTHERS PUBLISHERS
NEW YORK AND LONDON

WHAT MANNER OF MAN?

*Copyright, 1944, by Noel F. Busch*
*Printed in the United States of America*

*All rights in this book are reserved.*
*No part of the book may be reproduced in any*
*manner whatsoever without written permission*
*except in the case of brief quotations embodied*
*in critical articles and reviews. For information*
*address Harper & Brothers*

8-4

**FIRST EDITION**

**F-T**

This book is complete and unabridged
in contents, and is manufactured in strict
conformity with Government regulations
for saving paper.

E
807
.B837

TO
*Henry R. Luce*

FOR
VARIOUS REASONS
INCLUDING
THE AGREEMENT ABOUT DISAGREEMENT

71814

EMORY AND HENRY LIBRARY

# What Manner of Man?

# I

FRANKLIN DELANO ROOSEVELT
(pronounced rose'velt), 32nd President of the
United States of America, is sixty-two years old,
six feet one and a half inches tall, and 187
pounds in weight. He has blue eyes, large
freckled hands, and sandy hair which is gradually thinning. Roosevelt's health, on the
whole, is excellent although, like nearly everybody else, he is subject to colds in the head,
which, because of Washington climatic conditions, tend to settle in his sinus.

The President's inability to walk, in consequence of an attack of infantile paralysis in
1921, does not cause him pain nor does it
seriously discommode him. The President
wears leg braces which enable him to give the
appearance of walking when this seems appropriate. Ordinarily he moves about in a wheel
chair which he can propel himself although

he prefers to have someone, usually Arthur Prettyman, his valet, push him at the rapid rate of about five miles an hour. Speedy travel of all sorts pleases Roosevelt. He has special oversized casters on his desk chair, which enable him to shove it back with an abruptness that is useful both for transferring quickly to the wheel chair and for disconcerting callers.

Roosevelt's use of a chair to serve these two purposes is characteristic, as are both the purposes in themselves. His fondness for speed might be linked in his character to confidence, justified or otherwise; dependence on agencies outside himself; impetuosity; and enthusiasm for excitement. Likewise, his occasional willingness to startle someone sitting across the desk from him could be regarded as a function of his well-developed facility in self-expression; his interest in other people; and his friendly desire to have an effect on them or at least, and perhaps even more fundamentally, to attract their attention. By making a single, humdrum article of office furniture serve as a vehicle for both of these complex and allied motivations, the President is displaying compound, or grand-scale, ingenuity. Roosevelt's ingenuity is so pronounced that he has sometimes even been accused of being devious.

The President's fondness for grand-scale liveliness is shown not just by his office chair but by everything he does. For instance, he likes parties, especially big parties. On his birthday, he has not one, like other people, but two. The first party, held on his birthday eve, is a sort of curtain raiser for the multiple party at which, by means of Presidential Balls all over the United States, large sums are contributed to the National Foundation for Infantile Paralysis. At the small party, funds are contributed to a poker game in which the President traditionally engages with a few old friends, many of them newspapermen.

Poker, a game at which Roosevelt is both adept and diligent, also gratifies his fondness for excitement and ingenious, or devious, behavior. On one occasion, Roosevelt got so interested that he refused to end the game when it became time for him to go downstairs and make a fireside chat to the nation. Instead, he told the other players to wait for him; and to make sure that no one would help himself to his chips in the meantime, swept the whole stack into his coat pocket. During his chat attentive radio listeners heard an occasional crackling sound which, a little different from static, suggested that the Axis was trying to scramble the broadcast. This sound was made by the poker chips in the President's pocket, which he rattled from time to time by twitching his right shoulder.

White House poker games are usually dealer's choice. The host likes to deal and takes pride in contributing eccentric variations. After his radio chat, the President distinguished himself by inventing a variation in which each player got five cards to be picked up and five more face down on the table, the latter arranged in a criss-cross pattern which had something to do with the order in which they could be used. This variation proved to be so complex that the other players could not understand it at all and protested strongly when the President proposed a repetition. Roosevelt good-humoredly gave way to their insistence.

Poker games are of course a rare diversion. The only other evening amusement available to him, outside of pawing over his stamp album for a few minutes, is an occasional movie, shown in the White House projection room. The President likes mystery pictures or comedies, especially Walt Disneys made before their creator became military-minded. Items of this sort are likely to be recommended to him by his wife or by anyone else in the White House set who has seen one that seems likely to amuse him. The picture is then requested from a local exchange by one of the ushers. The President sits in the front row and delivers himself of critical or other asides when he feels like it in a fashion that would cause people in near-by seats to shush him if he did the same thing in a public theater. The President goes to the movies about twice a month, which is far below the national average. Ordinarily he puts in the evening working and then reads himself to sleep with a detective story around 11:30, unless some stay-up-late like Winston Churchill happens to be visiting. His taste in these is extremely catholic and even extends to ones that he has read before. On his trip to Teheran, he took along a box containing more than fifty, chosen for him by the Library of Congress.

If Roosevelt were subjected to a scientific aptitude test, it would indicate that he belongs to the small, fortunate category of human beings who are able to fulfill themselves quite completely in their jobs. His job consists chiefly of dealing with people. As indicated by the way he runs the government even more than by his fondness for poker

games and parties, there is nothing that the
President likes better. The President's liking
for people in general extends to his own family. He has five children—Anna, James, Elliott, Franklin and John, in order of seniority
—and fourteen grandchildren, whose names
are of no consequence, at least so far. None of
these are living at the White House although
most of them show up there when they get a
chance, but the President corresponds with
his children regularly, occasionally in longhand. His letters to his sons, who are all on
active service, may go by diplomatic pouch
but the President sometimes uses V-mail. The
President and his wife get along well together,
on a basis of mutual affection though not always complete understanding. Like everyone
else in the country, the President, despite his
own approval of sociality and swift motion, is
somewhat baffled by the lengths to which his
wife carries her own propensities in these directions. One night in the spring of 1943,
Roosevelt was working at his desk with some
advisers when Mrs. Roosevelt popped in: "I
just wanted to say good bye, dear."

"Where are you going?" asked the President.

"New York."

"But, dear, you can't do that. We have a reception at four-thirty tomorrow afternoon and then ——"

"Oh, I'll be back in plenty of time," said Mrs. Roosevelt gaily. "I just have an appointment in the morning, a meeting at Todhunter and then a luncheon somewhere . . ."

As Mrs. Roosevelt left the room, the President looked at his companions and emitted a low, expressive whistle.

Although puzzled by his wife's activities, the President regards them with complacency and rarely expresses even such mild irritation as that to which he was stirred on the night they were to attend a state dinner at the British Embassy in honor of the King and Queen's visit to the United States. Mrs. Roosevelt, already late, found she had got into the car without her scarf and had to go back for it.

"Honestly, Eleanor," the President called after her, "one of these days you will forget your head."

During Mrs. Roosevelt's frequent absences the White House is run by a kindly middle-aged lady named Mrs. Henrietta Nesbitt, who orders the food, arranges the menus, sends the laundry out, pays the bills, and handles the ration cards.

Mrs. Nesbitt, a resident of Hyde Park who had previously run the Woman's Exchange in Springfield, Mass., was engaged when Roosevelt first took office and has had her hands full ever since. Owing to the large number of people it contains and, even more, to their exaggerated goings and comings, running the White House is really less like running a normal home than running a small hotel or a good-sized ship. Mrs. Nesbitt, in 1933, hit on the bright idea of buying food from wholesalers to cut down expenses, thus doing her part at least to keep the President's promises about the national budget when he was first elected. Although the President's attitude on this point has changed with the years, hers has not and she still lives well within the allowance of $2,000 a month which comes from Roosevelt's salary of $75,000 a year. She also manages to make out all right with the ration cards, aided by the fact that the President prefers game and fish to red meat.

Mrs. Nesbitt runs her department of the White House from a cozy little office in the basement, which is otherwise given over mostly to storerooms and the two kitchens, which run sixteen hours daily. Various people buzz in and out of this office from morning to night, including the upper strata of servants, and ushers who keep her informed about how many there will be for lunch, where the meals should be served, and what everybody feels like eating. Of late, Mrs. Nesbitt's office, which is to the White House itself what the President's office is to the country as a whole, has been the scene of even more commotion than usual because of the servant problem, which is just as acute in the presidential ménage as it is everywhere else in the nation.

All White House servants have to be okayed by the U. S. Secret Service, which increases the difficulties. Like any good housekeeper, Mrs. Nesbitt usually hires friends of employees instead of going to an agency. In this process she is assisted by the circumstance that several members of the staff, like Arthur Prettyman and Elizabeth the cook, can qualify as old retainers.

According to one legend, the oldest servant in point of service the Roosevelts ever had was Mattie, a cook, who came to them more than twenty years ago. Mattie, whose constancy may be hereditary, is one of thirteen children of a Virginia mammy, whose mistress says that some weeks after Mattie left, she asked the mammy how her daughter was getting along. "Mattie's doing fine," said the mammy, "she's got a job working for a lawyer fellow in

New York and he likes her cooking, and she likes him very much, and they get along fine."

Several years later, the mammy's mistress again inquired about Mattie. "Doing fine," said the mammy. "Still working for that same lawyer fellow, and he likes her cooking, and they get along fine."

Ten years later, the mistress of the mammy brought the subject up again. "Why, Mattie's doing just fine," replied the mammy. "Still working for that same lawyer fellow, and he likes her cooking, and they get along fine. Only, they moved to Washington now, and they live in the biggest house in the United States."

In point of fact the White House is by no means the biggest house in the United States, to say nothing of England where, according to the celebrated Hudson River landscape gardener, Andrew Jackson Downing, a friend of Roosevelt's great-grandfather, there were fifty thousand bigger ones as long ago as 1850. The White House, so named because a coat of wash was applied to its brownstone exterior in an attempt to make it look respectable after British raiders burned the capital in 1814, is situated at 1600 Pennsylvania Avenue, the rather bedraggled street which ends a mile and a half farther south at the Capitol. Across this avenue from the White House drive is a meager little park containing an equestrian statue of Andrew Jackson, a few trees, a dozen or so resident squirrels and, occasionally, Mr. Bernard Baruch. Two years ago secret-service men closed the sidewalk in front of the White House for security reasons. This, combined with the presence of Mr. Baruch, created quite a squirrel problem in the park. The White House sidewalk squirrels moved over there in search of food and were so well-fed by Mr. Baruch that they settled down to stay. The problem was solved, however, when the President provided Mr. Baruch with a job justifying an indoor office and when, simultaneously, the secret-service men at the White House gates began to carry hazelnuts, thus causing the squirrels to move back and re-settle.

As distinguished from the squirrel population problem, the human population problem at the White House is complicated by the fact that the Roosevelts do not even have the use of the whole place, although they have the run of it. They live in effect in good-sized quarters on the second floor, just as a shop-keeper might live above his shop. The down-stairs part of the house, except for two dining rooms at one end, is mostly taken up by a ballroom and three reception rooms which are used only for public—that is, business— purposes.

In the twelve years of the Roosevelt tenancy the White House has acquired a special character. The grounds, which cover a total of about eighteen acres, seem rather incongruously cluttered up with secret-service men, wearing uniform or plain clothes. Several cars are usually parked outside the front door. At the side doors, under the portico, there is a miscellaneous litter of things like outdoor furniture, wood boxes, stakes, and Flexible Flyers used by Sistie and Buzzie Dall during their period of childhood residence several years ago. Sistie is now seventeen and Buzzie is fourteen.

The interior of the White House swarms with commotion and has an atmosphere somewhat like that of a railroad station and somewhat like that of domestic establishments like the ones in *You Can't Take It With You* or Sanger's châlet in *The Constant Nymph,* where anything may happen at any time. The swarming is accounted for partly by Roosevelts and their highly variegated friends or associates and partly by the staff, which has to be on hand to take care of these. The former group used to be more kinetic and explosive when the Roosevelt offspring were on hand. Pillow fights might then be going on in one part of the house while the President received a visiting cardinal in another and dogs, young married people, promising ballet dancers, youth leaders, and who-all were chasing or tripping over each other through the halls and corridors. Latterly, the situation has calmed down somewhat though formidable tides of humanity still rise and fall in more or less flood fashion throughout the day, leaving a high-water mark of hats and gloves, mops and dusters, old umbrellas, and other bits of flotsam. The White House staff, which only polices the flow of other people in King Canute fashion, is divided roughly into three categories: servants, secret-service personnel, and office assistants to the President. The office assistants, who form the smallest group, are composed of two dozen or so secretaries and secretaries' secretaries. The secret-service men, including indoor and outdoor types and plain and uniformed types, are about twice as numerous. The servant swarm varies, depending on how many extras have been called in, but there are usually twenty-five or so on duty in the daytime, all of them colored, of whom four live in.

Throughout the morning the White House

is filled with the kind of subdued clatter
which most men can hear only on days when
they stay at home from work because of illness, and which therefore has a vaguely reassuring quality, of brooms, vacuum cleaners,
dim telephones and doorbells, hallway gossip,
window opening and shutting, and sofa
thumping. At about eleven o'clock, this commotion is dramatically interrupted. In each
of the many rooms and corridors between the
President's quarters and his office a small elec-
tric buzzer rings three times. This is to warn
their occupants and the secret-service men on
duty along the route that the President is on
his way to work. The hallways, rapidly emp-
tied, become silent. A moment later, the President's wheel chair pops out of the door of his
room, whizzes into the elevator to the basement, races past Mrs. Nesbitt's cranny, and
shoots along the portico. Secretaries and assistants who have been talking with the President upstairs follow him along, at a walk that
is almost a dog trot, while the President turns
his head to address the rear guard of the scam-
pering procession in his loud clear voice.
Presently the wheel chair and its followers
pass through the portico door of his own office
in the White House annex. The door shuts

and the normal clatter of the ménage is gradually resumed.

When Franklin Roosevelt makes his matutinal arrival at his office, he has already been awake for two or three hours. The President has his breakfast, consisting of fruit juice, coffee, toast and scrambled eggs on a tray in bed at about eight o'clock. While breakfasting, he reads the papers—Washington, Baltimore, and New York first editions— to find out what has been going on in the world. Fala, his Scotch terrier, is allowed in the room at this time but cannot get on the President's bed because it is too high for him to jump.

Toward nine o'clock, Major General Edwin ("Pa") Watson, the President's aide, enters the room with a list of the day's appointments. These he reads aloud to the President, who approves most of them although he may change the timing slightly. Watson is likely to be followed by Stephen Early, James Byrnes, Harry Hopkins, or one or two others of a small and select group of advisers who are on terms of bedroom intimacy with the chief executive. Having finished his business with these, the President rises, performs his ablutions, shaves his large face with an old-fashioned, jackknife type safety razor and gets into his clothes, with the help of Prettyman. He has approximately thirty suits, most of them made for him by a Washington tailor, Rinaldi, along lines of the ready-made Brooks ones he used to wear when he lived in New York.

The President's journey from his bedroom to his office takes a bare three minutes, on the average. When he reaches his office he swings himself out of his wheel chair into the caster chair behind his desk and stays there almost continuously for the next eight or nine hours. About six days out of seven he has his lunch brought in on a wagon. In any case, owing to his inability to move around without considerable effort or assistance, he spends no time on the kind of strolling, window opening, stretching, or seeing visitors to the door that take up half an hour or more of the average executive worker's day. The President sees callers all morning. In the early afternoon he may see more callers unless it is Tuesday when he has his press conference, or Friday, in which case he goes to a Cabinet meeting. Late in the afternoon he gets to his mail, which has been winnowed down from the five thousand or so letters which the mailman brings every morning to the dozen or so which his secretariat really thinks he ought to see. To these the President dictates the answers, in most cases rapidly, without pausing for a word or correcting himself or having the shorthand read back to him by Grace Tully, the secretary who takes it. Really crazy crank letters amuse Roosevelt, such as one he got a year ago from a woman who said: "Dear Mister President: Just a few lines to ask you when people are divorced are they supposed to leave one another alone? My former husband is going around turning men against me with his lies. I guess he is mad because I gave myself to Red in the back seat of his car, License Number 247-895."

With callers and with his Cabinet, the President preserves an almost fabulously consistent amiability. This amiability is the chief ingredient of what is often described as the President's "charm." The fact that people are charmed by the President really derives from the far more important fact that the President is charmed by people—and that in being nice to them he is merely, sometimes, to be sure, unjustifiably, reciprocating their being nice to him. Since most people have been increasingly nice to Franklin Roosevelt and since he has always liked them increasingly on this account, it is not at all surprising that he has come to take their approval more or less for granted and become a real expert in making his approval apparent. Trying to decide which of the approvals came first is, of course, like trying to decide the same thing about the chicken and the egg, and need not be settled here. What is more to the point is the kind of charm which the President exerts, and whom it affects.

Charm is supposed to be an indefinable quality. This is because what charms some people repels others, so that no definition of charm can define all kinds; and also because, whereas some people may like a man for his charm, others may like him despite the charm, and for a different reason. The best way to get at the matter of Roosevelt charm is therefore to consider (a) the charm of animals in the zoo, since they have no other attraction and in their case charm is thus isolated from extraneous factors, and (b) to value in these terms the charm of some other public figure comparable to Roosevelt.

All public figures have some charm for some people, or else they would not be public figures. In the case of Wendell Willkie, the charm is that of the shopworn polar bear in Central Park. This scruffy bear, especially in spring or summer, manifests an amiable bewilderment. He waves his head from side to side, utters almost intelligible grunts while ambling in his cage, and seems to be worried, powerful and unhappy. These qualities tend to enlist sympathy for the bear among passers-by. Even on cold days, they say, "He looks hot and bothered."

Roosevelt's charm is not bear charm but seal charm; far from looking bothered, he seems alert, secretive and refreshed. The seal, trained or otherwise, always looks quite capable of dealing with any emergency; he seems to enjoy captivity more than his native habitat, if that is possible. He can do anything required of him, whether it is to catch a herring for his luncheon, balance a ball on his forehead, or play the national anthem on a set of horns. Urbane and indefatigable, the seal is the all-around animal, on land or sea, indoors or out, winter or summer. People who like the seal—they are more numerous than those who like the poor old polar bear—do so not for reasons of sympathy but from sheer envy which, repressed, amounts to admiration. Just so, Roosevelt especially charms those in whom friendly feeling is directed toward superiors; whereas Willkie appeals more to those who express love in the form of pity. As to the President's charm, however, whether he has seal blood or otherwise, there is no doubt that he has allowed himself to like, and to be liked by, many people whom he would have been much wiser to have thrown right out the back door.

Toward seven o'clock in the evening, charming ends and the President goes up to change for dinner. Before the war he used to get in a swim at least three times a week. Now, he is lucky if he manages even one, although his doctor, Vice-Admiral Ross T. McIntire, who has an office in the White House, proposes to improve his regime in this respect. The President took up swimming as a regular means of exercise after his illness, both because swimming was good for his paralysis and also because, in view of his paralysis, it was the only practicable exercise. In the water the President can, aided by its buoyancy, walk without support and does so to exercise his legs. He also swims about normally, using a crawl stroke and letting his legs drag behind him. Since his technique has improved by long practice, the President is a very good swimmer indeed and can rarely resist the temptation to duck or otherwise playfully molest anyone who happens to be in the pool with him and who would obviously be able to best him in a struggle on dry land.

On days when he fails to get in a swim, Roosevelt usually manages a massage. This is given him by Lieutenant Commander George Fox, who uses a special technique, digging his knuckles deep into the well-padded presidential exterior. Shortly before dinner, the President addresses himself to his cocktails. He takes about two a day, which he likes to make himself, often old-fashioneds with more bitters than would suit the average taste. While he downs his cocktails, Roosevelt puffs a cigarette, frequently the first of the day's second pack, through his whitish holder. The presidential cigarette holders are of a special kind, with a replaceable transparent interior that is supposed to do something to the nicotine. They used to be made of ivory but the supply ran out some time ago, and the President now uses a composition job that suits him just as well. Other kinds of cigarette holders, especially nonwhite ones, do not appeal to the President at all. People are forever giving them to him but he gets rid of them, along with most of the other useless knickknacks that arrive from well-meaning admirers all over the world.

As a gregarious man, President Roosevelt has many friends; as a man whose life is composed of his work, his friends naturally partake of it. Whether Roosevelt chooses his friends from among his working associates or gives jobs to his friends is a moot point but not, perhaps, worth debating. More consequential are the questions of what kinds of friends he makes and to what use he puts them. Roosevelt, it has been said, uses men where other more solitary, introverted types of executives might use books, as sources of information. He also uses them as agents, encouragers, amanuenses, stooges, sounding boards, amplifiers, court clowns, Cabinet ministers, and special deputies.

Roosevelt's tendency to surround himself with counselors, official and otherwise, was first spectacularly demonstrated just before the 1932 campaign when he assembled a group nicknamed the "Brain Trust," composed of Messrs. Raymond Moley, Hugh Johnson, Rexford Tugwell, Adolf Berle, and some others who have since passed into comparative oblivion, merciful or otherwise. Since then a dazzling cavalcade of such characters, some with official titles and some without, has passed through the White House. For a time the celebrated Thomas Corcoran, now a Washington corporation lawyer, and Benjamin Cohen, now a general counsel of the Office of Economic Stabilization, were the leading lights in the palace entourage. Other knights of the breakfast table have been Harry Hopkins, Felix Frankfurter, Admiral William Leahy, Stephen Early, Isador Lubin, Robert Sherwood, Samuel Rosenman, Sumner Welles, Leon Henderson, Emil Hurja, James Farley, and many another now forgotten.

The things that mystify people in general about Roosevelt advisers are (1) how Roosevelt selects them, since many of them are obviously of inferior grade; (2) what the advisers actually do; and (3) why the turnover among them is so heavy. The advisers themselves, as distinguished from people in general, are not at all mystified by the first two points, since they have some idea what they are doing and do not consider themselves of inferior grade. On the third point, however, their mystification appears to be even greater than that of the outside public, and all sorts of odd theories have been put forth to account for it.

A Roosevelt adviser who has been subjected to the brush-off often acquires a special kind of pathological mental condition which has now almost reached the status of a New Deal occupational disease. The precise form

it takes varies with the individual. Hugh
Johnson became sentimental. James Farley
became angry, Mr. Moley became critical,
though in a sympathetic way. In the reaction
formula of all the brushed-off intimates there
was a common denominator, however. This
common denominator was their bewilderment. All Roosevelt intimates have been
inclined to believe that their relations with
the President rested upon unspoken mutual
loyalties which made a brush-off unthinkable.
Thus, the brush-off, when it came, revealed
to them the fact that Roosevelt's understanding of the relationship was, somehow, different from theirs, and that a course of action
which seemed entirely extraordinary to them
did not appear at all extraordinary to him.
And the very fact that the President seemed
to have no sense of guilt about administering
the brush-off and none of the hostility a boss
usually feels toward a fired employee or of the
uneasiness such a warmhearted man might
be expected to feel about discarding a pal,
tended to make their bewilderment as intense
as the resentment which it partially replaced.

The state of mind experienced by brushed-
off Roosevelt advisers is best indicated by the
elaborate explanations which they themselves
think up in order to explain their predica-

ment to themselves. The most picturesque
and perhaps superficially accurate of these
explanations was recently provided by a
brushee who compared himself to a baby
thrown out of a droshky to a pack of wolves.
According to this theory, Roosevelt is a
droshky driver and the anti-Roosevelt faction
of the public are the wolves. When the
droshky, or administration, slows down or
encounters a heavy drift, the President simultaneously lightens the load and diverts the
wolves by pitching a helpless passenger over
the side.

Reminded that this process, while advantageous to the droshky and its driver, may,
in the scales of abstract justice, seem disadvantageous or even unfair to the wolf-bait,
the brushee altered his metaphor, choosing
a martial simile to account for the fact that
he himself felt no sense of having been be-
trayed. He explained that Roosevelt aides
are like the Marines at Tarawa. They enlist
for the duration and have sense enough to
consider themselves expendable. According
to this metaphor, the strategy of power politics sometimes makes it advisable, when hue
and cry is raised about some mess, to distract
attention from the mess and to imply that it
is being tidied up by blaming it on some

individual and then getting rid of the individual. Since the individual has taken the risk of being so utilized when he joins the palace entourage, he should not be aggrieved when called upon for a gesture of self-sacrifice which is, after all, less practically painful than it might be if there were not soft jobs in private life awaiting all discarded Roosevelt intimates.

This explanation of Roosevelt's attitude is plausible but romantic. The true state of mind of a Roosevelt brushee was perhaps best defined by the most famous of them all, James Farley, in a conversation with his doghouse roommate, Mr. Hurja. Hurja said, "All the same, if he asked you to come and have lunch with him, I'll bet you'd do it." "Yes," replied Farley, "I would—but I'd make a statement on the White House steps after lunch, saying that he had asked me."

One way to get at the kind of people the President does like is to rule out, first, the kinds he doesn't like. This is not so easy as it might appear because Roosevelt seems, superficially at least, to like all types. Still broadly speaking, it is obvious that he does not feel especially attracted to, or at home with, older men, or any men of very pronounced views which are in opposition to his own.

There is certainly nothing startling about the second point. Everyone prefers to associate with people who are loyal and sympathetic. Men in positions of executive responsibility feel this need not less, but more than other people: (a) because they like to have their decisions corroborated and (b) because they need to have their decisions carried out without argument. All executives therefore tend, quite properly, to surround themselves to a greater or less degree with what are called "yes-men"; and the more they use people in their work the more yes-men they require. This situation, though generally satirized, is in line with common sense; for an executive to surround himself with "no-men" would simply make it impossible for him to do his work. Nor is it fair to assume that all yes-men are docile stooges, rather than willing assistants. It is true that there have been among presidents some exceptional ones who liked to have some no-men among their associates, Lincoln, for instance, placed a high value upon the counsel of Seward. It is also true that Roosevelt is not such an exception, and that his yes-men are perhaps a little more docile and a little more lacking in qualities other than the capacity for agreement than would be ideal.

As to the lack of older men, this is not surprising either. The age differential between the President and his father, James Roosevelt, was such that as a child he was discouraged from turning to that parent for companionable advice. It was thus inevitable that in later life he showed no habitual reliance on, or affinity for, older, more authoritative persons. Parenthetically it should be added, lest the point be counted for more than it is worth, that had the President been otherwise conditioned and had he, like most men, preferred to be a protégé or to occupy a position of subservience he would, also like most men, be occupying one now, rather than the White House. And it should also be noted that, from time to time, the President has had congenial relations with his elders, like Bernard Baruch, the late Cardinal Mundelein of Chicago, and his old headmaster Dr. Peabody. However, these rare individuals have—perhaps also in the Roosevelt family pattern—stood to the President more in a grandfatherly than a paternal relationship; and none of them have been a dominant, or constant, influence.

Having ruled out the kind of people the President does not want around him, the next step should be a study of the ones he does want. Since the death of Louis Howe, the President's closest associate, not to use the word "friend," has undoubtedly been Harry Hopkins. Their intimacy began when they met as fellow campaigners for Al Smith in 1928, ripened at the time Hopkins became executive director of the New York State Emergency Relief Administration in 1931. Before meeting the President, Hopkins had never displayed any marked ability. The President, however, discovered in him talents so great and so diversified that they seem literally infinite, and no one has yet tried legally to define them. The United States government made no provision for a job that would entail such varied activities as the spending of incalculable millions of public funds, on the one hand, and chatting privately with the dictator of Russia, on the other. To call Hopkins a mere super ambassador-plenipotentiary would be as absurd as to call him a mere economic royalist on a scale never before imagined. In fact, he is far more than both of these rolled into one because he has been many other things as well and, although seriously ill at present, may be something else tomorrow. Hopkins has shown considerable competence to justify the President's confidence in him. The question is: on what was the confidence based? Hopkins is a chatty, nervous, reassuring sort of man, with a profound sympathy for the underprivileged.

Next to Hopkins, the most influential adviser of the President has probably been Felix Frankfurter, an Austrian immigrant of Jewish parentage whose mother encouraged his vigorous and well-rewarded efforts to rise, by sheer social and intellectual volatility, from the squalor of New York's East Side to the eminence of a Supreme Court justice. Frankfurter further embellished his reputation as a fearless Liberal by his highly vociferous participation in the Sacco-Vanzetti case. A frantically gregarious intellectual, he made himself valuable to Roosevelt by sending swarms of protégés to Washington in the early days of the New Deal. On reaching Washington himself, far from discontinuing his social life, he naturally extended it.

Frankfurter's personal intimacy with Roosevelt appears to have begun to cool about the time the former, on reaching the Supreme Court, attained prestige which had previously been denied him. This fact, in itself a considerable clue to the character of the President, Frankfurter and human nature generally, has not prevented the little judge from exerting a perceptible torque on the affairs of the nation. His views, or more properly his wishes, still permeate the capital as a whole, and the President's clique in particular. Thus even when he thinks he is seeing someone else, the President is in fact often seeing Frankfurter as it were in disguise.

Roosevelt's most recent protégé is Edward Stettinius, an agreeable and handsome young man who has the title of Under Secretary of State. The President's enthusiasm for Stettinius, who had been made Chairman of the Board of the U. S. Steel Company at the age of 37, first developed about 1940 and was looked upon in some quarters, like his earlier enthusiasm for Averell Harriman, the young Chairman of the Board of the Union Pacific Railroad, as an example of a new presidential warmth toward "businessmen." The fact is that both Harriman and Stettinius were not only businessmen but business prodigies and both had reached their juvenile eminence through rather special circumstances. Bluntly, both Harriman and Stettinius were less businessmen in their own right than the sons of businessmen. The difference between a man who so violently rebels against his environment, or so wholly dominates it, that he creates a great fortune and a man who so wholly accepts his environment as to follow in his father's footsteps is, barring contrary evidence, as profound as the difference between a tiger and a tabbycat. Such sons of businessmen are primarily sons, and thus make ideal protégés. Stettinius, a well-mannered and broad-minded youngster whose economic views have a liberal tinge, has shown himself an acceptable replacement for Sumner Welles, whose "divergencies of policy" had previously offended the gnarled old Secretary of State, Mr. Cordell Hull. Mr. Hull never expressed any enthusiasm for the intimate relationship which used to exist between Welles and the White House.

Possibly the strongest figure in the President's present entourage is Admiral William Leahy, a hard-bitten, quiet and enormously competent old sailor whose intimacy with the President goes back to the Wilson administration. Leahy is both an older counselor and the furthest thing from a yes-man that could be imagined. However, a look at the rest of the entourage suggests that Leahy's possession of these qualities is an exception so startling that it can only be viewed as the proof of a rule. The President's two literary jukeboxes, Archibald MacLeish and Robert Sherwood, have lately been less conspicuous at White House tête-à-têtes but both were on hand over a long period. Both substantiate the impression that the kind of associates the President likes best are talky, sympathetic, idealistic ones, like the woolly Mr. Wallace, with whom the President replaced John Garner; the ubiquitous Isador Lubin, who is the current White House domestic chore boy; the erudite and amiable Judge Rosenman; and most of the rest of the contemporary Kitchen Cabinet.

The President came to like Leahy, whom he met during the last war, before his acceptance of, and enthusiasm for, oral personalities was as fully developed as it is at present. Almost the only comparable case is that of Donald Nelson. Although not a White House habitué, Nelson has been given considerable authority by the President, directly or otherwise. Nelson is a hard-shelled businessman of the type so rarely preferred by Roosevelt that it is practically nonexistent in Washington; however, its very rarity worked in Nelson's favor because it permitted his thin protective disguise—that of being a lenient, easygoing drone—to pass undetected. Since being tardily recognized by Roosevelt underlings for what he really is—a hardheaded boss so sure of his authority that he does not need to pound his desk—Nelson has, of course, lost some favor; and the argument against him made by oral personality types, who are by definition skilled in argument, has been precisely on the ground not that he was too "authoritative," but that he was not authoritative enough. Evidence of Nelson's deficiency in this regard has been that he failed to fire "incompetents" in his organization. Nor is it odd that Nelson's view of what constitutes incompetence should differ radically from that of talky, rival executives who spend their time adducing the evidence.

Nelson is a case in which the instinct of the President himself, as reflected in the instincts of his subordinates, for picking talkers went completely haywire, for understandable though ironic reasons. Such instances are extremely rare, however. More customary are cases of the reverse procedure, of which the most dramatic was perhaps that afforded by the late General Hugh Johnson. Johnson looked like a man of action if ever there was one. He ranted and raged, had a high military rank, and thought himself quite capable of running not merely one business but all the businesses in the country and he set out to prove it.

Megalomania of this type is to be associated with the deep oral personality and quite often brings its efforts to deal with reality to

such abrupt conclusions as that of the Blue
Eagle in the sick-chicken case. However, it
was interesting to note that, when finally
placed in the crucible of circumstance and
melted down, Johnson turned out to be just
a newspaper columnist, which is to say the
epitome of the chatty type. Nor was this
eventuality any less surprising to the public
because Johnson had spent many years of
his early life in writing adventure stories.
This preliminary clue to the real virtues of
his character had been concealed by Johnson's
eagerness to draw attention to the façade with
which he hoped to conceal it later on.

Even more extraordinary than the Roosevelt brush-off is the Roosevelt treatment of
babies in the droshky who mew unhappily
when the wolf pack snaps at them. The
whole country has wondered for twelve years
why the President has never fired Frances
Perkins, whom he seems to regard as a faith-
ful and well-meaning governess. Another
presidential adviser once asked Miss Perkins,
why, when even the Kitchen Cabinet was
wondering when Roosevelt would shake off
Hugh Johnson, the President did not do so.
"You know," said the Secretary of Labor
thoughtfully, "he has a great instinct for
these things. Something like this situation

came up in New York one time. The President waited for three or four weeks, and the man died. All our problems were solved."

In Johnson's case, the man was less accommodating. Roosevelt finally offered him a job as head of a great international commission, studded with big names. "In other words, you want me to quit," said Johnson, and wrote a two-and-a-half page resignation, full of forlorn reproaches. The President replied in longhand, refusing to accept it, and kept Johnson in his job for five months longer.

Although the President conceives of his job in terms of friends, he rarely moves his private friends into positions of public authority. Henry Hooker and Langdon Marvin, his successive law partners; Lathrop Brown, his Groton classmate and Harvard roommate; and Edmund Rogers, whom he played with as a whippersnapper—all these are still good friends to the President but he has never given them government jobs; nor has he offered one to Vincent Astor, with whom he used to like to go yachting.

On the other hand, since the President puts so much of himself into his own job, friendly notions about his fellow workmen are likely to pop into his head at almost any moment. Some years ago, while listening to a speech at a Jackson Day dinner, the President's face assumed a brooding look. He leaned over, tapped John Garner on the shoulder, and said, "Jack, if anything happens to me, I want you to take care of Pa Watson for me. He would like to be ambassador to Belgium." Nothing happened to Roosevelt but something did happen to Jack Garner. As for Pa Watson, not long ago he was made a major general.

Of course, to people who are not only outside the presidential ring but also out of sympathy with it, the whole entourage has a most alarming aspect. Real businessmen, who hate the sort of person the President likes, naturally regard his associates as dangerous, without really knowing why. On the other hand, real labor leaders, of whom John L. Lewis is an example, are even more alarmed than the businessmen. Lewis, as a strong, paternal type, is also the sort of man for whom the President has no liking, for the same reasons that he is not fond of most heads of business—who of course dislike Lewis also. The pattern of disaffections naturally leads to frequent misunderstandings.

What makes the presidential entourage genuinely alarming is not that the President's taste in people is, if possible, more inclusive than his taste in storybooks. It is that, unlike the storybooks, the people are not there for purposes of recreation only. The truth is that what the people want is power; this the President gives them, in enormous quantities. Unself-confident people often try to do all their own work, and several other people's also. This may make them bad at delegating work to others and inferior as executives. Highly self-confident people often get other people to do their work for them and, especially in democracies where popularity pays off well, are much more likely to achieve executive political positions. In general, this is all for the best, but in extreme cases the arrangement has some disadvantages. An extravert like Roosevelt is not only so ready to delegate work that he delegates his own, like drafting speeches, he is so generous that he delegates the same job to several people, and so warm-hearted that he hates to withdraw these signs of favor.

Boiling it down, the President tends to govern through subsidiary executive bodies; these bodies tend to be headed by people of his choice; and his choice tends toward talkers rather than doers. These talkers tend to select more talkers as their own underlings. Thus the whole chain of command from the White House down operates not to penalize but to reward executive incompetence, an arrangement that seems all the more deplorable since the most notable feature of the Roosevelt administration is that it calls for more executive ability than any other president's scheme, and more for executive ability than for anything else. This, however, is a perfectly natural sequence of events. It may not have disastrous consequences.

# II

To ATTEMPT a commentary on Franklin Delano Roosevelt in the year 1944 argues temerity on the part of the author for two major reasons. On the one hand, so many comments have already been made about the President that it seems arrogant to add another, unless from a fresh point of view. On the other hand, a reader might well suppose that the only fresh point of view conceivable about Roosevelt would be that of retrospect, which is, as yet, impracticable. Temerity is occasionally justified, however, and the reasons for essaying a new study of Roosevelt may possibly outweigh those against it.

The object of such a study is to give the reader some insight into the subject's actions. If these actions are of influence, the insight may do more than gratify an idle curiosity.

Roosevelt's actions not merely influence the 131,000,000 people in the United States more than any other single person's but they also have a perceptible effect on the two billion or so other human beings scattered around the world. Consequently, any new light that can be shed on them should have a passing value.

Roosevelt's actions, like everyone else's, may sometimes puzzle people. This creates the illusion that they are inherently puzzling and that the motivations for them are not only difficult but perhaps impossible to ascertain. In fact, Roosevelt's actions, also like everyone else's, are expressions of his character. The reasons for them all are to be found there.

On the face of it, this may not seem to clarify the matter greatly. People have been talking for centuries about the mystery of human personality, and so forth and so on. Consequently, since people believe what people say, people have fallen into the habit of assuming that the human personality in general or in particular is an extraordinary riddle. The truth is, however, that, if any mystery at all exists about the human character, it is largely the kind of mystery which a multiplication problem might present to someone who did not know arithmetic. That is to say, if one applies the correct procedure, the mystery will vanish and an answer will be substituted. Of course, it should be realized at the outset that to understand a character is not necessarily to be able to predict its future actions; because these are affected by exterior conditions which are irrelevant and unforeseeable. Roosevelt himself is well aware of this, as he showed one day while making cocktails in the White House. Asked by a friend what kind they would be, he answered brightly, "Wait and see. You know, I'm unpredictable."

In Roosevelt's case, two special conditions do indeed tend to increase his unpredictability. One is that the exterior circumstances which affect him are both more numerous and more sizable than usual. The other is that, although an understanding of his character is more worth while than an understanding of most other characters, it is peculiarly difficult to apply the correct method. Thus in order to understand a character, one should first of all be in possession of a large number of facts. Where Roosevelt's is concerned, for somewhat the same reasons that make the understanding important, these facts are more or less inaccessible. Consequently, our understanding of his character will necessarily remain somewhat incomplete; but it should be understood that this is due not to inadequacies in the procedure but merely to technical difficulties in applying it.

All this may make it sound as though some sort of secret formula were in the offing. Nothing could be further from the fact. Human beings are creatures of habit, from the cradle on. Once one knows how habits are formed, and how they alter and merge with each other through the years, it is not at all hard, if one knows what a person has been up to over a fairly long period, to see exactly what his habits consist of. These habits—emotional, moral, physical—constitute his personality. A knowledge of them enables us to see that his actions are not an amazing welter of complex and contradictory impulses but a logical, even an inevitable, series of responses to environment. It is a simple matter of research and common sense.

Parenthetically, it should be added that the method is not an appealing one and that this very fact tends to corroborate its soundness. Most people have early in life formed the habit of admiring or hating other people and therefore insist upon doing one or the other. On the contrary, the habit of understanding people is extremely rare and, from the literary point of view at least, not nearly so profitable as regarding them as heroes and villains. It is perhaps a pity that when one understands a person he inevitably turns out to be neither a hero nor a villain. Indeed, the very terms themselves belong to romance and our world of habitual illusion.

To get back to Roosevelt: Many of the facts of his life are fairly familiar to everyone. But these facts have all been put forward piecemeal and apropos of day-to-day news. Furthermore, when grouped at all, they are usually synthesized to support an argument or a point of view of some illusory sort. What it amounts to is that, though we hear more about Roosevelt than anyone else, we know less about him, since what we do know is presented in such a way as to increase the confusion. The following pages represent merely an effort to explain Roosevelt as completely and as dispassionately as possible.

The procedure began with an examination of where the President is at present. It will continue with an examination of how he got there. If this process is executed successfully, the result will be a superimposition of past upon present which should give an

effect somewhat like that achieved by looking at a photograph through a stereopticon.
That is to say, the President's character will,
as it were, assume three dimensions instead
of two, and the reader may know something
that he did not know before.

To begin at the beginning entails talk
about heredity. Franklin Delano Roosevelt's
heredity was excellent. Founded in America
by a Dutch peasant named Claes Something,
who took the name of Roosevelt (Rose field)
because that was the name of the flowery
village he had come from, the Roosevelt
family presently produced more presidents
for the United States than the Hanovers have
produced kings for England. According to
genealogical charts, Claes Roosevelt was the
common ancestor of James Madison, Martin
Van Buren, Zachary Taylor, William H.
Taft, Ulysses S. Grant and Jefferson Davis
as well as Theodore and Franklin.

In addition to presidents, the Roosevelts
produced other interesting offshoots. Claes
Roosevelt had two grandsons: Jacobus, from
whom Franklin is descended, and Johannes,
who was the forefather of all other branches
of the family. One connection produced the
president of the first Bank of New York which
Joseph Alsop and Robert Kintner, Roosevelt-

family journalists, call the city's oldest banking house. Another collection went to Paris and got into the works of Proust. Others mingled, largely with each other, in New York City drawing rooms or upstate New York country houses. Since there were so many Roosevelts and since they were respectable enough to lead lives of comparatively public record, it is possible to decipher certain qualities which all had in common.

Roosevelts are sane, gregarious and healthy. These three qualities tend, of course, to go together. Stock which produces nervous, measly members may furnish geniuses or idiots. But sound extraverts like the Roosevelts habitually like, seek out and marry others of their type. The Roosevelt habit of intermarrying with Roosevelts is not a symptom of inbreeding; by the time it developed, the clan was so numerous that the degree of removals of cousinship had grown almost astronomical. Thus, when Helen Roosevelt, Franklin's half niece and the daughter of his mother's stepson "Rosey," married Theodore Douglas Robinson, nephew of Theodore Roosevelt, whose niece Eleanor married the present President, it made the Robinson son Douglas sixth cousin, second cousin, and half first cousin once removed to Franklin

Roosevelt's daughter, Anna. To complicate
matters further, Roosevelts not only became
presidents but undersecretaries of the navy
—Theodore, Franklin, Robinson, Theodore,
Jr., and Henry L. Roosevelt.

Established early in the fragile, flexible
United States aristocracy, the Roosevelts did
not need or wish to take part in the industrial
upheavals that produced a new and gaudier
branch of this aristocracy late in the nine-
teenth century. This is one reason why the
members of the clan were thrown together,
along with Astors, Vanderbilts and small fry:
it also helps to explain the background of little
Franklin. Hyde Park, which his father bought
in 1867 where he was born and reared, is
really not much of an ancestral manor house,
even in Dutchess County terms, compared
to elaborate establishments like the Her-
man Rogers or Frederick Vanderbilt estates.
There, however, his father, James Roosevelt,
retired early and lived quite enjoyably, breed-
ing trotting horses until he bred the best one,
Gloster.

To members of the flashier Oyster Bay
Roosevelt clan, which mixed with upstart
Wall Street rich on Long Island, politics sug-
gested noisy posters, wards and Tammany.
Theodore Roosevelt's father was properly

shocked when his eccentric son plunged into such a milieu. To the old-fashioned Hudson River Roosevelts, politics were on a different plane, and simply meant the White House. Cleveland offered James Roosevelt a legation, which was natural since James liked traveling in Europe and often summered at Bad Nauheim. James declined but paid a call on his old friend in Washington. Franklin Roosevelt's first visit to his later residence was thus made in company with his father. Cleveland, worried by conditions, patted his five-year-old successor's head and said, "I hope you'll never be president of the United States."

To say that character is the result of heredity and environment is misleading. Actually, heredity merely supplies the marble which, while essential, is less necessary to the statue than the sculptor. For character, the chisel is environment; and so far as heredity is concerned, Franklin Roosevelt had got all he could get out of it when he let out his first yowl, and a loud one. It is therefore appropriate here to consider not what effect heredity had on Franklin but what effect he will have on it. In view of Roosevelt contributions previously made in this direction, all Roosevelts naturally look on the Presidency as a sort of family business. Franklin and Eleanor

Roosevelt would be inhuman if they did not occasionally wonder which of their promising brood is likeliest to go into it.

So far, Elliott, James and Anna seem to have partially disqualified themselves by divorce. John, now a lieutenant in the navy, is still undeveloped. Franklin, Jr., however, may be on the track. Decorated for heroism and recently promoted to Lieutenant Commander, he has been mentioned as a governor for New York after Dewey. This does not mean that Eleanor Roosevelt consciously raised her boy to be president. Such presumption would be less proper in her case than in that of Franklin's mother, who, when a friend asked whether she was not surprised to realize that her son was living in the White House, replied, "No, why? It is just what I planned."

Roosevelt as a small boy was greatly devoted to his mother. This fact has been noted by all his biographers. Some of them have placed a favorable interpretation on it, pointing out that it showed the goodness and sweetness of his character. Others have reached the conclusion that he was a "mother's boy," a "sissy." The matter requires considerably more attention than it has yet received, since the impressions of a human being in the first years of his life must determine his future character, at least to the degree that they set the pattern for his reactions to all later impressions.

There is nothing mysterious about this. It is merely to say that an infant or small child notes what happens to him and draws his conclusions of cause and effect therefrom. Since what happens to him is usually determined by his father and mother, their attitude toward him, and his toward them, will, in a fundamental way, decide his future reactions to everything else.

The whippersnapper Franklin Roosevelt was interested in boats, and fond of a certain tree house. Putting these items together, any parlor psychoanalyst can discern substitutes for the prenatal state, and argue that Roosevelt's devotion to his mother was exaggerated. In ⁻ fact, the items cited are substitutes for the prenatal state; but so also are such childish devices as swings, pillow caves, high places, express wagons, sleds and God-knows-what-all, not to mention such adult devices as houses, automobiles and yachts. That, no doubt, is why Roosevelt liked them; if so, it is also why all other children and adults like them or their equivalents. The fact is that it is difficult to find in the recorded

history of Roosevelt's infancy and early childhood any symptoms of abnormally extreme
attachment to his mother. Furthermore, such
an attachment is usually accompanied, if not
indeed caused, by strong hostility to a father
and there is no evidence to show that little
Franklin entertained such hostility. However,
no two bent twigs, and no two children, grow
up exactly alike; and in view of what was to
become of him later, it may be worth while
to note a few points about the Roosevelt
ménage in the decade that started on January
30, 1882, when little Franklin made his first
appearance.

Roosevelt's position in the family was not
that of only son, in the ordinary sense; he had
an older half brother, James (who died in
1927), the issue of his father's first marriage.
But he was his mother's only son. An ordinary
only son gets the undivided attention of both
parents and is disposed to develop certain special good and bad character traits on this
account. An urchin situated like young Franklin is not a less special, but a more special,
case than an ordinary only son, because, while
he divides the attention of the chief parent,
he gets the exclusive attention of the other.
While it may be surprising that Roosevelt's
relations with his mother were not overtly

closer than the record shows, in view of the circumstances, it is certainly not surprising that his relations with what psychiatrists call mother-substitutes are still both close and special.

The United States electorate is in probably one sense, as a source of sustenance, approval and protection, a mother-substitute, for Roosevelt and for all other men in public life. Roosevelt, however, justifiably or otherwise, feels that he has a stronger claim on this beneficent body than all other public men and all other presidents—and he has enforced this claim. It must naturally have seemed to him not so much extraordinarily agreeable as, simply, suitable that in the large confraternity of presidents he should be the only one favored by a third term. And this attitude helped him to secure this special dispensation.

One reason Roosevelt liked his mother so much was that she liked him so much. A lady of strong character and warm affection, she was in age about halfway between her husband and her child, and treated both in a wise, companionable way. Most of the available material on Roosevelt's childhood, and certainly the best, is that contained in a book by this distinguished old lady written when she was 79, after Franklin had been elected president. The book is interesting not only for the incidents it relates per se but also because the incidents which Madame Roosevelt chose to recall are inevitably indicative of her own attitude toward her son.

One of the earliest incidents in Roosevelt's childhood is one that he himself has apparently retold as his earliest memory, showing that, whether or not it is his earliest memory, it was traditionalized as such in family lore. This incident concerns a crisis on board the liner *Germanic,* in the year 1885, and it involves a small jumping jack. While returning from Europe, the *Germanic* encountered heavy seas. A great wave broke over the ship and water poured into the Roosevelts' stateroom, washing the jumping jack, Franklin's favorite toy, onto the floor. Franklin was not dismayed by the water or the excitement. He enjoyed them both but was concerned about the toy. "Save my jumping jack, save my jumping jack!" he cried. The jumping jack was saved.

For the fact that this incident was preserved in the Roosevelt lore and that Roosevelt himself consequently considers it his first memory it is easy to find a superficial explanation. The wave that flooded the Roosevelt cabin also damaged some of the ship's gear and forced it to turn back. The episode therefore constituted a real crisis in the grown-up lives around him and his part in the drama would naturally come to mind in a grownup's reminiscences. At the same time, one can detect another reason for the legend's durability. A sensitive and companionable mother would have been aware that her son had personified his lively little toy and perhaps identified himself with it in the way that children properly do. She would also have approved heartily of his generous impulse to pull the helpless little creature out of the water. Roosevelt's mother, a member of the closest thing to a ruling class that the United States affords, was strongly motivated by the spirit of *noblesse oblige* and she encouraged such evidences of this feeling as were exhibited by her son.

Likewise, in the company of parents who had always shielded him so completely from danger that he had not re-encountered it since birth, it was natural that Franklin should have felt no fear of a mere ocean wave, even a big one, in his cabin. Indeed, the fact that it was in the cabin rendered it doubly innocuous because his father and his mother were in the cabin also. The whole thing must have been pleasant and the fact that his parents

were excited made excitement pleasant also.
Roosevelt may have got his love of excitement in general and marine excitement in particular from the wave incident, or he may have had it already, in which case the wave confirmed it. In any case, the President always enjoys commotion and is never inwardly disturbed by it. He just wants someone to retrieve the jumping jack, or Poland.

The memoirs of Madame Roosevelt show that young Franklin early identified himself with authority. However, lest these memoirs be taken too seriously, one should remember that in compiling her book, with the aid of ghost writers, Mrs. Roosevelt was justifiably putting what she considered the best face possible on her story; and also that, at the period when little Franklin was growing up, *Little Lord Fauntleroy* was an international best seller. At the same time, the story of a certain governess is valuable evidence. While in Paris, the Roosevelts had imported this governess from Vienna. When she arrived, it developed that the governess was unsatisfactory for reasons which the author fails to go into but which may have been connected with the fact that governesses rarely seem entirely satisfactory to mothers who have only one son. When Mrs. Roosevelt consulted Franklin as to how he liked his supervisor, the little boy gave a noncommittal answer. Time went by, further instances of the governess's failings appeared, and Mrs. Roosevelt interviewed Franklin on the subject a second time. On this occasion, Franklin stated that the governess was dreadful. Asked why he had not said so in the first place, he replied:

"I thought after you and father had gone to such trouble to get her, it wouldn't be right for me to complain."

According to Mrs. James Roosevelt, little Franklin was usually the leader when playing with his small pals. This shows the confidence in meeting the world which he had derived from his successful encounters with it even earlier. When asked why he felt obliged to lead, the future president replied, "If I didn't give the orders, nothing would happen." True or false, this answer displays not only acumen typically Rooseveltian, but eagerness for action.

The reason Roosevelt preferred sailboats to quieter replicas of the cradle was probably that boats move dangerously and encounter wind and storm. If winds and storms are lacking, other boats may provide even livelier disturbances. Once as an adolescent, Roosevelt undertook in the Bay of Fundy to hail a schooner whose captain said he was carrying potatoes from Canada to Maine. "Chinese potatoes, I suppose you mean," shouted Roosevelt, correctly guessing that the schooner's cargo was illegal immigrants. The captain was disgusted, but chose not to show it. On another occasion, Roosevelt was given permission to board the Kaiser's yacht, lying at anchor in a Norwegian fjord. When the amiable monarch merely looked at him, Roosevelt went so far in his effort to stir up a crisis as to steal from a cabin desk a pencil which he had sized up as the Kaiser's favorite since it bore his toothmarks. Some boys may have been sent to jail for smaller misdemeanors. Life was kind to Franklin Roosevelt and did not snub his eagerness.

By and large, the main thing to be learned about Franklin from his mother's book is that, in a far more subtle and effective way than the one currently recommended by advanced, experimental schools, she not only helped his ego to grow but adroitly guided its development. She encouraged him to talk and listened sympathetically when he did so; Franklin thus acquired a considerable faith in the power of words, especially words spoken by himself, which has never deserted him. She surrounded him with love, attention and friendly people. Since she was his world, he thus conceived of the world itself as a friendly and attentive milieu. It has not, so far, entirely disabused him of this concept.

Roosevelt was educated at Groton, Harvard and Columbia Law School. He did not, however, go to Groton until he was fourteen and consequently about half his prelaw-school education had already occurred before he got there. This part of his education is usually dismissed in his biographies by the statement that he was taught by a succession of tutors, as though the matter ended there. The fact is that it did not end there at all. Education by tutor is, in the United States, an extremely unusual process. There is no reason to suppose that the effects of this unusual process upon Franklin Roosevelt were especially negligible.

For the benefit of those who were educated otherwise, the role of a tutor in a family like the Roosevelts should be explained. The tutor is a young man of genteel background and education, who lives in the house and acts not only as teacher but also as companion to his charge. He combines the roles of father, older brother, and male nurse with that of pedagogue, and thus plays an enormously important, if not indispensable, role in the charge's doings. This is especially true if the charge has few friends of his own age, as must be the case if he lives on a large estate up the Hudson where the nearest neighbor is a long walk from home. It is even more true if the little boy's father is, however friendly, much too old to be regarded as a boon companion.

Roosevelt's father, his age dramatized all the more by contrast with the lively young mother, must in little Franklin's mind have occupied the place which, in the minds of most small boys, is occupied by a kindly and indulgent resident grandfather. The role of father, as generally understood, was perhaps much more nearly filled by the tutors. While they may resemble fathers in some important ways, tutors differ from fathers in even more important ways. A father represents authority, often disagreeable authority, in an immediate and also in a final form. In Roosevelt's case, James Roosevelt may have represented authority in a final form but the immediate representative of authority was the tutor. The crucial difference between the authority of a father and that of a tutor is that, whereas a mother may be overruled by a father, the tutor may be overruled by the mother.

In short, Roosevelt's major encounters with male authority, which determined his eventual responses to authority in general, were cushioned and modified. Indeed, he encountered authority, of which the essence is that it be sovereign, in such a nonsovereign form that he may be said not to have encountered it at all. However, since the tutors did have nominal authority over him, the fact that they usurped the place of true authority was to some degree disguised from little Roosevelt himself; and so, although he had not really encountered authority, he behaved as though he had. Thus Franklin showed good manners and obedience. And the fact that his tutor was not merely an occasional dramatic influence, as most fathers are, but a steady and ordinary influence, like a friend, tended all the more to make him at ease in the presence of sovereign authority because he was ignorant of its possible painful effects, as these are understood by most healthy extraverted little whippersnappers of his type.

Another important point about Roosevelt's tutors, wherein they also differ from the fathers who perform their functions in most households, was precisely the fact that there was a series of them. From time to time a tutor left or got fired, by maternal edict, and was replaced by another one. This interchangeability of tutors too worked to diminish whatever awe small Franklin may have felt about them; and it also set up a sort of behavior pattern at the age when such patterns are most easily effected. When he needed to know something, Franklin asked the tutor, one of whose functions was to tell him things. When he wanted to do something, the tutor was supposed to help. And this arrangement worked out very well.

On one occasion, while visiting in London, Franklin Roosevelt tried to get into the South Kensington Museum on a day when a select garden party was being held at which the Prince of Wales was guest of honor. He had with him a special life membership card in the Museum of Natural History which his grandfather had procured for him as a reward for making a collection of birds from the woods at Hyde Park. With mischievous, and entirely praiseworthy, disregard for the august nature of an organization which to most small boys might seem to be an almost overpoweringly solemn embodiment of empirical majesty, and also for the proper purpose of his grandfather's present, Roosevelt slipped this card to the tutor. By means of some hanky-panky with the doorman, who had never before encountered any such credentials but assumed they were adequate, the tutor got himself and Franklin into the reception.

On another occasion, while Franklin and a tutor were touring the Continent, they contrived to get themselves arrested four times in a single day, for minor infractions of civil regulations. The arrests occurred in Germany, long before Roosevelt's encounters with Hitler or his small theft from the Kaiser. Both episodes are striking demonstrations of the fact that even when far from home, where he might have felt himself at something of a disadvantage, and even in vulnerable childhood Franklin Roosevelt's attitude toward authority was one of such extreme, almost disdainful, confidence that it can best be explained on the basis of nonrecognition. Furthermore, in both cases his tutor, far from being even faintly associated with the side of the ruling power, was actually an accomplice in Roosevelt's spry and ingratiating circumventions.

Roosevelt's close association with tutors ended when he went to Groton. At Groton, and later at Harvard and Columbia, his teachers stood more or less in the same relationship to him as the tutors had formerly stood. Shortly after he went into politics, Roosevelt felt the need of a tutor again and speedily got himself one, in the person of Louis McHenry Howe, whose close and specialized relationship with Roosevelt political writers found so difficult to define; and who was later made not a general but a Kentucky colonel.

The way in which Roosevelt regarded his tutors was no doubt patterned after and conditioned by his relationship with his older brother, James, nicknamed "Rosey." This would have been inevitable in any case, since Rosey was in the same age bracket and had always acted in the same general advisory capacity as the tutors, and was the only person whom Roosevelt had previously met of such age and function. Rosey, enough older not to regard Franklin as a rival but not too old to be a crony, liked his small half brother enormously and treated him less in an authoritative than a companionable way, just as Roosevelt confidently expected to be treated, and accordingly was treated, by the tutors.

Just as the tutors had replaced Rosey, Louis Howe was replaced after his death by Harry Hopkins. By this time, however, the President had realized that there was no reason why tutors should not run in tandem rather than team formation. He had surrounded himself with tutors on every conceivable subject, from literature (Judge Rosenman) to global strategy (Admiral Leahy). Roosevelt, being friendly and animated by *noblesse oblige*, always hated to see a tutor, or a governess, leave. Still, to dispense with a tutor when his services, either as an accomplice in outwitting authority or in some other connection, were no longer essential naturally aroused in him no more feeling of guilt than he now feels about the fact that most of his present tutors receive their pay from the national treasury, just as the tutors of his childhood got theirs from its parental equivalent. Mrs. James Roosevelt's private fortune, of roughly a million dollars, was about twice as big as her husband's.

In a democracy like the United States, a successful career in politics calls for a great variety of superficial techniques which the politician demonstrates, and his critics examine, so diligently that they serve to conceal the basic aptitudes from which the techniques derive and without which the techniques would be useless as well as unattainable. Thus, to start with, a successful United States politician must be a reasonably good talker; he must like people; and he must be ready and willing to accept responsibility.

Roosevelt's close association with his mother, who considered his every word a jewel, ensured his ability to fill the first requirement. In his sheltered childhood the only creatures he encountered—relatives, family friends, servants or domestic animals—

either liked or revered him. This gave him, by reciprocity, deep faith in human nature and took care of the second point. Franklin Roosevelt's early adjustments to authority, as necessitated by his relations with his father and his tutors, took care of the third. Consequently, he was a twig so bent as to be quite capable of growing into presidential timber by the time he entered Groton school. At Groton he demonstrated his capacities, on the one hand, and was encouraged to develop them in new directions, on the other.

Roosevelt's development at Groton was in a new direction because here for the first time he was on his own. The general effect, like that of removing a plant from a hothouse into the garden, was at first retarding but later advantageous. To understand precisely why this should have been the case one must know more about the kind of place it was.

One of the characteristics which United States critics flay most diligently about the British scheme of things is the influence that the old school tie has in the government. The critics assert that, because of the excess valuation placed upon such haberdashery, second-raters get into positions for which they could not qualify on merit. Nonetheless, whatever the old school tie may prove about the British government, it proves one thing about the old schools: they are at least an integral part of the British scheme of things; and since their whole purpose is to train boys to run the country, it is certainly not their fault if too many of the boys eventually do so.

In this respect, British public schools differ vastly from United States boarding schools. Our boarding schools are, to be sure, copied from British public schools, but our system of government is not copied from the British system of government. Consequently, even though they greatly resemble British schools in all the nonessential features of curriculum and atmosphere, American boarding schools, for precisely this reason, utterly fail to resemble their models in the crucial feature of supplying members of the governing class— which is not surprising, since we have none.

In other words, while the British government can be accused of containing too many old school ties, American schools can be accused of not furnishing the government with enough graduates who amount to anything, either in the government or, for that matter, elsewhere. Groton and Exeter are the only big American boarding schools that have ever produced any presidents. That Groton has produced such a lively one is in part a tribute to the admirable methods of its founder and first headmaster, the Reverend Endicott Peabody, who at least encouraged the idea of public service along British lines and who gave the school its motto, "Whose service is perfect freedom." It is also, in even greater part, a tribute to the character of Franklin Roosevelt, who did not fit into the boarding-school pattern especially well and who was, perhaps just for that reason, all the better equipped to fit into the pattern of ordinary American life, which he encountered later and elsewhere.

Franklin did moderately well at Groton, but the school did not afford the kind of rich topsoil to which he was accustomed. For one thing, he started at fourteen in the third form, whereas most little Groton boys start at twelve in the first form, like little Eton boys. This meant that Roosevelt, who had never had contemporary brothers, let alone playmates, now encountered large numbers of playmates who were of two varieties, older and younger. The masters were a more familiar type, in so far as they resembled his tutors; but to the degree that he acquired face with the masters, Roosevelt lost face with the students and his general perceptions about dealing with people were by this time sufficiently sound to enable him to sense the flaws in this arrangement.

Roosevelt chose a wise mean in his adjustment. He stood near the top of his class, played football on the scrub team, excelled in a minor Grotonian athletic specialty—the "high kick"—and kept his authority identification dusted off by acting, in his last year, as baseball manager, with the help of four assistants. Roosevelt's enthusiasm for talking to an audience was gratified when he joined the debating club. His enthusiasm for saving things, already projected on a much larger screen than that of his counterpane, was gratified when he took the affirmative in a debate on the subject of granting freedom to the Philippines. His love of excitement was frustrated when, having run away from school to fight in Cuba, he came down with measles and wound up in the school infirmary. All in all, however, the main advantage of Roosevelt's sojourn at Groton was that there, for the first time, he encountered real resistance to his inclinations, albeit of a genteel and miniature sort. The wonder was not that he failed to excel his classmates but that, instead of being thwarted and intimidated by the abrupt change in his relations to the world, he made the best of them.

The way in which hale human beings deal with resistance is to contend with it. Roosevelt contended at Groton as a competitor against his fellow students, in scholastic, athletic, managerial and verbal fields. He also contended against circumstance in general, as is indicated by the fact that he did not become either a prefect, a top scholar or a football hero, like those less fortunate little boys who respond so completely to the special Groton environment that the larger environment of United States civilization never seems quite satisfactory by comparison.

When Roosevelt went on to Harvard his newly acquired acceptance of the competitive principle helped him to display his other proclivities to the best advantage and thereby to develop them further. Roosevelt began by running for the *Crimson*. In the capacity of reporter he was quite as undismayed by real, major domestic authority as he had been by symbolic, minor foreign authority in his childhood. At the beginning of his freshman year, Roosevelt felt capable of bearding the president of the college, to ask whom he was going to vote for. He did this so blandly that the late great Dr. Elliot told him, thereby giving Roosevelt a national scoop which was republished all over the country. A few months later, when his distant cousin Theodore Roosevelt, then vice president, came to Harvard to lecture, Franklin got a collegiate scoop on the event, thus upsetting a precedent whereby such visits were to be unpublicized.

The editor emeritus of the *Crimson* was elected to the title of president. Roosevelt acquired this presidency, his first of any sort, in his fourth year at Harvard. Nothing about the experience gave him any horror of the title. Indeed, the reverse occurred. As president of the *Crimson*, Roosevelt indulged his lifesaving and crisis-seeking proclivities to the full. Most college editors choose dull subjects and hold forth either about campus problems, which are important but on which they cannot speak their minds, or on world problems, about which they know nothing and on which they can have no influence. Roosevelt, apt always in the major matter of his choice of subjects, hit on a campaign against inadequate fire precautions in Harvard dormitories. He handled this subject with such vehemence that it seemed to be a major crisis in the affairs of the yard and succeeded in having fire escapes and safety devices installed.

The fire escape campaign was merely Roosevelt's contribution to local improvement. He was, of course, busy on the world scale too. His activities on this plane took the

shape of fund collections to support the bel-
ligerent Boers in South Africa, one of whose
generals, Jan Christian Smuts, was later to
function as a sort of occasional stand-in for
Roosevelt's side-kick, Winston Churchill,
who was in the same war as a correspondent.

At Harvard, Roosevelt worked out with the
crew squad more as a matter of physical exercise than of athletic competition. Instead of
studying books, he began collecting books
about the Navy. In his sophomore year he
joined the Fly Club which, with Porcellian,
is ranked as one of the two best for Harvard
undergraduates. However, far from subscrib-
ing to collegiate social standards, Roosevelt,
even more emphatically than at Groton,
tended to ignore them. As his social circle
widened, it grew deeper. He associated with
scrubby, casteless classmates from the Boston
suburbs. Like the grooms' and gardeners'
children at Hyde Park, they seemed more
exotic and more lively than his own set, of
which, however, he was also fond.

During most of Roosevelt's undergraduate
career at Harvard, his mother lived in Boston.
This was less extraordinary than it has been
made to seem by some commentators; James
Roosevelt had died in 1900 and there was no
special reason why his widow should have se-

cluded herself in the lonely house at Hyde Park. To his mother's Boston house Franklin brought his classmates and friends. It was noticeable that he had none of the reticence about letting his friends perceive the close attachment that still existed between him and his mother. On the other hand, Franklin did show reticence about letting his mother perceive the close attachment that developed between him and someone else—his distant cousin Eleanor. Indeed, his reticence on this subject was such that he did not mention the matter at all until he and Eleanor had become engaged, in the fall of his senior year.

Mrs. Roosevelt, so far as one may deduce from both her immediate and her later behavior, justified her son's reluctance to inform her on this point by a repressed sense of injury which she did her best to keep politely concealed. As a matter of fact, surprise at this development, which was the form she chose as the overt outlet for her state of mind, might have been lessened had she realized that in choosing a cousin whom he had known since he was four, and even a cousin with the same last name as herself, her son was in fact paying her a subconscious compliment of considerable value. Nor was his willingness to keep his marriage, so far as this is permissible at all, "within the family" contradicted by the ceremony itself on St. Patrick's Day, 1905. Franklin's old headmaster officiated and the President of the United States gave away the bride, who was his niece.

While Franklin finished his education by studying law at Columbia, then a much more elegant sort of institution than it is at present, he and his bride lived comfortably, though not ostentatiously, in a house on East 36th Street, which had been furnished and decorated by Franklin's mother. Franklin failed to get a law degree but passed his bar examination, which enabled him to start practice as a clerk in the firm of Carter, Ledyard and Milburn, at 54 Wall Street. Some of the President's biographers have suggested that failure in this office, or at least a dislike of Wall Street formed at this time, accounts for Roosevelt's later attitude toward business in general. There seems little reason to accept this hypothesis.

The truth is that, for the four years or so after leaving Harvard, Roosevelt was looking about to find a suitable outlet for his stored-up energies. Carter, Ledyard and Milburn did not cause him to dislike Wall Street. He disliked Carter, Ledyard and Milburn, along with Wall Street, already and for perfectly discernible reasons. In order to feel a brotherly or friendly attitude toward people it is necessary to be animated by the same incentives—a fact which helps to explain, among other things, why sovereign nations fail to get along well with each other. With his fellows in school Franklin had always got along well because there he had the same incentives in the form of approval from masters, the student body, *et al.* In the great world a rift suddenly opened between young Roosevelt and his contemporaries, especially in Carter, Ledyard and Milburn. This was due to the fact that a new element—money—had entered the picture.

For Wall Street people, whether they have much of it or not, money is the prime incentive. For Franklin Roosevelt, who had never given the matter much thought, money was no incentive at all and consequently he and his colleagues failed to find common ground. This misunderstanding was dramatically exemplified one morning when Mr. Ledyard, a regular economic royalist of the old school, found Franklin mooning about the reception room, and began to ask him questions. Roosevelt, characteristically eager to have Mr. Ledyard like him, though for friendly and not mercenary reasons, naturally answered "Yes, sir, yes sir," to the senior partner. On this occasion "yes" was inadequate as an answer. Mr. Ledyard, who was seeking information, rather than approval, became amazed. "Roosevelt, you're drunk," he said and left the room.

Roosevelt was not drunk, but he presently became discouraged. He took to spending longer and longer weekends at Hyde Park, nourishing his fiery love of crises in rather forlorn symbolic fashion by joining the Hyde Park Hook and Ladder Company. Roosevelt's presence at Hyde Park and his membership in the company, brought him to the attention of the local politicos who, in the Summer of 1910, were looking for someone naïve enough, on the one hand, and respectable enough, on the other, to accept the nomination for state senator from the Twenty-sixth District—a thankless honor because there was no possible excuse for expecting the recipient to get elected. Franklin Roosevelt seemed a likely sucker. The bait was extended to him at a conference of party bigwigs in Poughkeepsie one day in October of 1910 and Roosevelt swallowed it, hook, line and sinker.

". . . I think we can lay down a rule covering a political career entered into with the highest purpose of serving one's community or one's country. Either the individual should have enough money of his own safely invested to take care of him when not holding office . . . or else he should have business connections, a profession, or a job to which he can return from time to time."

This explanation of why so few first-rate people concern themselves with the job of governing the United States, and consequently why the country is rarely governed in a first-rate way, was made by Franklin Delano Roosevelt many years ago. The explanation is discerning, but a shade too bland. The number of individuals who ever have enough money safely invested "to take care of them" is extremely small; and no one who has engaged seriously in professional life, on a competitive basis, regards it as something to which he can "return from time to time" with any hope of succeeding even to the degree necessary to enable him to succeed more noticeably elsewhere. That is why major politicians in the United States are divided roughly into two classes: those who enter politics comparatively late in life after having made a success at something else, and who therefore really lack any strong incentive to make a success of their new career, and those who, having undertaken politics as a whole-time career in defiance of the Roosevelt rule, have such a strong incentive to make their careers successful that they cannot afford to take many risks.

Although in proposing his rule Roosevelt does not seem to be aware of the fact, he himself was in an extremely favorable position in regard to a career in politics. In having, practically speaking, no obligation to make his career a success, he was to be sure no better off than any other fortunate young man of independent means who may choose to enter politics. What Roosevelt had in addition were two other, less obvious qualifications for climbing the political ladder. One was that at the age of twenty-eight he had, in effect, been practicing politics at home, at school and in college for twenty years and thus had not a 20- but a 40-year advantage over men who reach politics belatedly, after dabbling in other fields. And the other was that no one in the political world was aware of this fact, which gave him the tactical advantage of complete surprise.

In sizing up Roosevelt, the political leaders of the Twenty-sixth Senatorial District had seen in him a well-to-do, extremely handsome and apparently public-spirited young man who probably knew little enough about politics to be tricked into accepting a thankless chore. The chore they had to offer was especially thankless. The state senatorial nomination had already been turned down by Lewis Stuyvesant Chanler, who preferred to run for the inferior office of state assemblyman. The reason Chanler turned it down was that, for the Assembly, he had to carry only Dutchess County whereas for the Senate he would have had to carry Putnam and Columbia counties too. If Chanler, a well-known and experienced campaigner who had been Democratic candidate for governor two years before, doubted his own ability to carry the three counties, it is not hard to guess what chance the party leaders thought an unknown novice would have of doing so. They congratulated themselves on getting young Roosevelt to take on the job, not because they felt that he had any chance of winning but because they knew that they were very lucky in adding to the ticket a respectable young man so naïve that he would not later expect to be reimbursed politically for losing.

The fact that, in persuading Roosevelt to run for state senator, the political powers of upstate New York were in the position of a snapper fisherman whose bait is swallowed by a shark did not become immediately apparent. Indeed, Roosevelt's first steps tended to corroborate the wrong impression that the bosses had of him already. The young man, instead of campaigning modestly as befits a novice soon to be painfully enlightened, made himself as conspicuous as possible. Automobiles were then a rarity in upstate New York. Roosevelt hired a bright red one, drove about the district at a high rate of speed, and delivered three speeches to his confident opponent's one, lest anybody fail to notice him.

Much has been made of the Roosevelt automobile and of the energetic campaign he made in it. This maneuver did indeed show his appreciation of the fact that the first thing to do in politics is to secure at least the attention of the electorate. More important, however, is the fact that, before accepting the nomination, Roosevelt took the pains to examine the situation more carefully than had the Poughkeepsie political leaders. In doing so, he saw what was plain enough to any sensible amateur but what they, in professional attention to technical detail had overlooked. This was that upstate New York voters would probably rebel against the Republicans for the first time in a generation as a result of disgust with the Taft administration in Washington and several other special circumstances. In fact, New York voters did precisely that and Roosevelt got into office by a narrow squeak of 1140 votes.

In this he was doubly lucky, both to win where a few votes cast the other way would have defeated him, and to win with a trend. If Roosevelt had won against the general trend, political leaders in the state might have valued him at his true worth long before they did. On the contrary, since a lot of other Democrats from Republican counties got in at the same time, Roosevelt's victory, which in reality showed political strategy of the first order rather than the mere tactical cleverness that would have been argued by victory against the trend, was really not counted in his favor at all. This meant that he still had the card of surprise up his sleeve. Presently he played it, to the best advantage, in the celebrated case of Blue-Eyed Billy Sheehan.

Cut down to its essentials, the case of Blue-Eyed Billy Sheehan was as follows: Charles E. Murphy, boss of Tammany Hall in New York City, found himself obligated to put up Sheehan as his candidate for senator from New York. Sheehan, a sort of hard-shelled, conservative Democrat, firmly identified with the "bossism" that was then as now being roundly condemned by editorial writers, was a weak candidate. Murphy, however, expected to put him across by means of a special system. Senators in those days were elected by the state legislature. The procedure was to hold a party caucus whose members would then be obligated to vote for whomever the caucus chose. Murphy knew that he had a majority of the caucus. Thus all that was necessary was that at least 101 of the 114 Democrats in the legislature attend the caucus, since this was the number of votes required to elect the senator. In due course the caucus was assembled and the noses counted. It was then found that several persons were missing from their seats—among them 18 Democratic assemblymen and one Democratic senator. The senator was Roosevelt. What had happened was that Roosevelt, having decided for reasons of his own that Sheehan was not a satisfactory senatorial candidate, had instituted and led a revolt against Mr. Murphy's project.

The reasons that caused Roosevelt to take the stand he took against Murphy and Sheehan have been analyzed extensively. However, since no one was inside his head at the time, the analyses are not altogether satisfactory, and in cases of this sort it is sometimes wiser to inspect the circumstantial evidence.

This shows that Roosevelt was not beholden
to Murphy for his election and that he had
nothing much to lose by opposing him, unlike
the leaders of the Sheehan faction, of whom
one of the liveliest was young Al Smith. It
also shows that Roosevelt had a great deal to
gain by opposing Murphy and that he did
indeed gain it. What he had to gain, since
Sheehan was a candidate for senator and Murphy a major-league boss, was primarily a
national reputation as a fearless independent
Democrat; furthermore, there was nothing to
fear in any case, since the reward for defeat
was glory also.

Most accounts of this episode describe the
wrestlings with his conscience which Roosevelt was obliged to undertake before his
conscience triumphed over his sense of advantage so far as to enable him to take the
bold stand which he did eventually take.
In fact, it would be more generous to
suppose that whatever wrestlings may have
been going on in the Roosevelt mind must
surely have been as to whether he should
really sacrifice poor old Sheehan to build up
a reputation on his own account. If his conscience was involved at all it must have been
as a charmed spectator, slightly inclined perhaps to a pious hope that charity toward a bad

old man rather than greed masquerading, however plausibly, as self-sacrifice would be declared the winner. If this was the case, the Roosevelt conscience was disappointed.

What happened was that Roosevelt and his rump caucus stayed out on a sort of sit-down strike, so variously motivated on the part of the mere assemblymen that Roosevelt, whose name and whose membership in the Upper House would have made him its leader in any case, naturally became their leader. His rented house in Albany—few senators can afford such a luxury—became its capitol and forum. Murphy has been accused of stupidity in not realizing the nature of his opponent; indeed, had he realized it, he would certainly have backed down in the first place by nominating someone else, as he was forced to do in the end. However, on the record up to that time, Murphy had every reason for supposing that Roosevelt was an extremely silly young man who knew nothing at all about politics.

After the episode of Blue-Eyed Billy Sheehan no one ever again mistook Roosevelt for a political nobody. In revealing his talents and his confidence in them, the future president had made himself a national figure. All he had lost, besides the possibility of surprising anyone in this direction again, was any chance of attaining the esteem and regard of Charles E. Murphy; but there would have been small chance of his acquiring this in any case, and furthermore he did not want it.

Roosevelt objected to bosses in politics less perhaps on principle than on even deeper grounds. Throughout his career he has always been a leader of the underdog party but always in a very upperdog way. At a snobbish college, he liked the proletarian element; in a Republican state, he was a Democrat; as a Democrat, he was against entrenched leaders. This is a part of the apparent duality of his approach to life, which derives from the unusual adaptations of his interesting childhood and makes his motives so mystifying and enigmatic to many people. Roosevelt is, as it were, for authority on the tutor level where he is against it on the paternal level. But even here he is not so much against ultimate authority as he is the representative of modified authority. And this is why he always disappoints the mothers' boys of the extreme left just as consistently as he disappoints their opposites on the extreme right.

After the episode of Blue-Eyed Billy Sheehan had brought him to national attention, Roosevelt did not find it hard to get re-elected and then to attach himself to the entourage of another anti-boss Democrat, in the person of Woodrow Wilson, just then being boomed for the presidency. Meanwhile he ran the Forest, Fish and Game Committee in the Senate and made friends with Howe, who was a former New York *Herald* race-track writer and liked to bet on futures.

When Wilson was nominated, Roosevelt stumped New York for him and rounded up a claque of two hundred to howl "We want Wilson" at the Baltimore convention. These services, in which his oratory was perhaps less useful than his name, deserved a reward. Josephus Daniels, a newspaper publisher, may have had a mild sense of the ironic suitability of offering Franklin Roosevelt the post of assistant secretary of the navy from which his distinguished cousin had started out on the road to the Presidency sixteen years earlier. It is a little naïve to assume, however, that Roosevelt took it just because he liked ships, though he certainly did like them. He had also been offered the job of collector of the Port of New York and that might have involved ships also. What he really wanted was a Washington job and a desk near the center of things, where there might be a crisis. The Navy seemed to fill the bill, and he jumped at it.

# III

AMONG the complaints occasionally heard about Mr. Roosevelt are those based upon the ground that he is a poor executive and untrained in this department of his job. This seems to be a serious charge, since he is supposed to be the head executive of the whole land, but it appears more serious than it really is.

In the first place, such is the nature of a democracy that, by definition, the chief executive must be selected less on the record of his executive achievements than on the quite separate record of his ability to convince people that he is a good executive. The public may find the house of a good mousetrap builder but it can scarcely be expected to run good executives to earth in their offices and then to haul them out to run for president. The truth is that any man who wants to be president must give so much time to telling people that he would be a good one that he rarely has much left over for proving this contention in any normal sphere, let alone one comparable to the White House.

In the second place, so far as any young man of presidential caliber can afford to prove himself competent to run a major desk, Roosevelt did so in the years between 1913 and 1920. It would be absurd to argue about just how well he did his job, or to make out a case that its administrative requirements were much like those of his present one. Still and all, confronted with a totally new sort of situation, he showed marked talent for adjusting himself to it, which is the main thing; and in so far as this new situation called for the exercise of judgment and the ability to take or give direction, he deported himself well.

In the hierarchy of Washington jobs the assistant secretary of the navy occupies a special niche for various reasons. One of these is that the admirals who run the Navy rarely have much respect for their liaison man with Congress; another is that the Navy secretaries are usually delighted by the admirals and want the admirals to think well of them. The consequence of this arrangement is that often while the secretary is making up to the admirals, and being amiably encouraged in the illusion that he is an old salt, the business of the department is attended to by his assistant. Josephus Daniels was a more competent secretary than some of his followers but no exception to this general rule. Navy men soon found it expedient to do much of their real work with his proxy. The knowledge of naval history which Roosevelt had acquired through his collection of old manuscripts on this subject, and the knowledge of boats he had acquired by sailing them, were not really relevant to the subjects in hand. However, they did give him a certain familiarity with seagoing jargon and enabled him to avoid making a fool of himself in conferences about naval matters, both rare talents for a man in his position.

So far as Roosevelt was concerned, the job had many other advantages. For one thing it permitted him to learn about Washington from an ideal situation which was neither so exalted as to prevent his seeing what made the wheels go around nor so menial that he was obliged to turn them by himself. By now equipped with three of their five children, he and his wife took a house on N Street and became social favorites. Some of the acquaintances struck up by Roosevelt, like that with

Leahy, stood him in good stead later. Others had a more questionable influence on his subsequent activities. In any case, Roosevelt found his new authority agreeable. When World War I turned up, making his job much more important than it had been, he found it more agreeable still.

One of Roosevelt's first Navy chores was to reorganize and improve yard installations and repair facilities along both coasts. Another was to work up, from material supplied by the admirals, the arguments for bigger appropriations which Daniels would present to Congress. A third was to let out contracts, order supplies, and otherwise superintend the spending of most of the money Congress authorized. He did all these jobs well—much better, for example, than his successor, young Theodore Roosevelt Jr., who, as Franklin later took occasion to point out, was only exempted from blame in the oil scandal of the Harding administration by his demonstrable ignorance not only about the scandal but also about everything else that the department had been up to generally.

When the war started, Roosevelt had to use his judgment as to where to build cantonments for embarkation points, what kind of guns to manufacture, and what kind of inventors to discourage and what kind to employ. Stimulated by his sense of crisis, Roosevelt pitched into all this with extraordinary energy and praiseworthy common sense. On one occasion, a bedraggled scientist sneaked into his office with a weird-sounding scheme for manufacturing mines with tentacles which were supposed to be laid undersea and thus keep Germany's submarine fleet bottled up in the North Sea. Roosevelt, pleased by odd specimens of humanity, permitted this eccentric to speak his mind at length. Then, having made up his mind that the plan was sound, he called it to the attention of Daniels, who called it to the attention of the Admiralty in London, who, after considerable shilly-shallying, consented to let it be tried. The mines with tentacles were a great success and did indeed bottle up the submarine fleet, just exactly as the eccentric inventor had predicted.

After the United States got into the war, the center of the crisis, so far as Roosevelt was concerned, appeared to be in Europe. Accordingly, after making unsuccessful efforts to get there in uniform, to superintend the installation of naval guns on land mountings, he went there as a kind of tourist, to inspect naval doings in the war zone. The trip, made on a destroyer, was a junket of the first order, and Roosevelt enjoyed it hugely, all the more because a certain atmosphere of danger and desperation surrounded the voyage. This atmosphere indeed eventually obscured the incident itself in Roosevelt's memory. In 1943, his naval aide asked one member of the party that accompanied him on the destroyer—by this time a high ranking officer in the navy—to write an account of the journey, describing their hair-raising encounters with such German submarines as had not yet been bottled up by the tentacle mines. The officer replied that he would be delighted to oblige except that there had been no encounters with subs, hair-raising or otherwise.

Late in 1918, the President went abroad again, to supervise the disposal of naval paraphernalia in France, and to tour the battlefields with his wife. This time he came back not on a destroyer but on the *George Washington*, on which Woodrow Wilson was his fellow passenger. The absence of a pseudo-paternal branch or box on Roosevelt's association-chart had by this time been well-demonstrated. He had had no favorite professors, no avuncular friends in professional life and no political patrons. On the whole,

this lack of habitual need to depend on older
men probably helped to develop, while it
also displayed, his feeling of independence
from authority. At the same time, it had some
disadvantages. These were shown in his relationship with Wilson.

Wilson was probably the closest approxima-
tion to a hero whom Roosevelt encountered
in his whole life; and it is thus noteworthy
that, given many a chance to see Wilson, he
never knew him intimately. Wilson himself
was not, of course, an especially paternal type,
but he was well-disposed toward young
Roosevelt and it is thus particularly significant that their shipboard association in 1919
did not ripen on dry land. All Roosevelt got
out of it was Wilson's desk and chair, for a
souvenir, after Wilson, for whom tragic defeat
was already in view, returned to his increasingly gloomy solitude in the White House.

When Roosevelt became the candidate for
vice-president the next summer, and went
with James Cox to call on the President at
the White House, it was Cox who caught the
spark of Wilson's vision and promised to
campaign on the League issue. If, in his
talks with Wilson at an enormously crucial
moment in the older man's campaign for
a new world, Roosevelt had really grasped

the point that by staying out of the League America˙ was in effect cheating itself of the victory for which the war had been fought, he concealed the fact in his campaign speeches. These seemed plausible but somewhat perfunctory arguments for a cause which he appeared to regard as justifiable and noble, rather than practical.

Up to 1920, Roosevelt's career had been a steady and rapid ascent. In the summer of 1920, his nomination for the vice-presidency climaxed it. The ensuing defeat might well have started a down curve which, long before 1944, would have put Roosevelt back at Hyde Park as a retired lawyer with a commendable public record. That nothing of the sort happened was in part due to a second and really unpredictable mishap, which occurred the following year.

Shortly after the campaign of 1920, Roosevelt joined with Grenville Emmet and Langdon Marvin, in whose offices he had previously maintained a desk, to form the firm of Emmet, Marvin, and Roosevelt. Then, to fortify himself for his new and not especially exciting duties, he set off on a yacht belonging to his friend Van Lear Black, who had also given him a $25,000-a-year job in his in-

surance company, to have a holiday at Campo-
bello. While out sailing with his family, he
sighted a small forest fire burning near the
coast. Roosevelt, a fire buff since his Harvard
campaign about buckets, reached characteristically to this crisis, by plunging swiftly into
it. He spent the day clearing breaks in the
path of the flames and wetting down the
underbrush where breaks were impracticable.
Late that afternoon, exhausted after a day of
unaccustomed exercise, he went for a swim
in the cold water of the Bay of Fundy. Then,
his physical vitality exhausted, he went back
to the house; there, partly because he felt too
tired to climb the stairs, he sat down on the
porch in his wet bathing suit to read the
afternoon mail. That evening when he went
to bed he felt as though he had caught a
heavy cold. The next morning the paralysis
had set in.

Poliomyelitis is still a little-known disease.
Opinions vary as to why Roosevelt caught it,
and what its effects have been. Some supposi-
tions are permissible, however. In the first
place, the fact that Roosevelt had been un-
usually healthy up to that time is not merely
an ironic incongruity. The fact is that people
who undergo small illnesses from time to time
tend, quite often, to escape severe ones. In

part this is because their bodies develop resistance by the very process of throwing off minor ailments. In part it is because, frequently reminded of the frailty of the human system, such people are inclined to take better care of it. How little the overconfident Roosevelt thought about his own health can be seen from the fact that, in the first days of his vacation and, surprisingly for a man who had spent so much time outdoors, he made precisely the error which tenderfoot campers or new arrivals at Palm Beach are liable to make —overdoing at the start. After a week or two in the woods, he might well have been able to put in a day of arduous fire-fighting and to feel all the better for it. After months in the city, the effect was to drain his resistance far below normal and to make his body a receptive vehicle for whatever infection happened to be handy. A mild epidemic of paralysis had been noted in New York that summer; and Roosevelt, in common no doubt with thousands of other adults who failed to contract the disease, had picked up the germs.

The question of why Roosevelt caught infantile paralysis is of less practical importance than its effect on him. He himself once summed up his views on this subject by saying, to someone who asked him how he managed to survive the strain of the Presidency, "Once I spent two years lying in bed, trying to move my big toe. That was the hardest job I ever had to do. After that, anything else seems easy." Even this may be to some degree an understatement. Not only did Roosevelt's illness give him a new conception of his own abilities, it also changed and amplified the abilities themselves. His career before the paralysis was that of a promising young man who had made reasonably good use of the exceptional opportunities which had been offered him. After it, his career was that of a man who made unprecedented capital out of an apparently calamitous infirmity. When it occurred, the illness appeared to be an internal explosion guaranteed to wreck his career. Instead, it proved to be a sort of rocket which, as the career began to slow down, gave it a vast new impetus that sent it far higher than it showed any signs of going in the first place. How and why this came about is worth noting.

Loss of the use of one's legs has several effects on the human psyche. One is that, when deprived of the power to move around, the mind demands a substitute or compensation for this power, such as the ability to command other people to move around. That is why almost all invalids tend to be peckish and demanding. However, to an adult of responsible and fatherly nature who remains bedridden for three years no such feeble response to the stimuli would suffice. Roosevelt sublimated and refined the pardonable peevishness of the normal invalid into an administrative urge which would have had profound consequences for him even if he had never become president.

This compensation, however, concerns only such loss of locomotive power as a man might suffer if both his legs were broken and failed to knit properly, or if he endured chronic gout. In Roosevelt's case an additional factor tended to reinforce and corroborate the purely psychic aspect of his illness. In addition to being useless to him, his legs also ceased to demand wages from his physique in the form of nourishment and glandular activity. More or less relieved from the necessity of taking care of his lower extremities, his internal machinery was thus able to do a sort of supercharged job on the rest of his physique, including the brain. It is an obvious fact that, since his illness, Roosevelt's face, once of a delicate cameo quality, has become large and bull-like. According to doctors who have examined him, his chest, once almost delicate, now can expand more than Jack Dempsey's. Though not so massive as it seems by comparison with his shriveled legs, Roosevelt's torso is, in fact, much larger than it was before 1921. And though his legs now weigh much less than they did, his total weight is thirty pounds over what it was when he was in college. The point of all this is that much of the vitality that used to go into Roosevelt's legs now goes into his superior members and results not only in an enlarged chest expansion but also in enlarged thinking capacity. Whether the thinking is done in the right direction remains a matter of opinion; but it is indisputable that more of it is being done than previously. Indeed, judging from Roosevelt's case, one might be justified in saying that infantile paralysis, far from being a handicap, would be a better treatment for doctors to recommend to businessmen who lag in middle age than useless, arduous golfing.

Impelled by immobility and encouraged by added mental voltage, Roosevelt's positive response to his paralysis was further emphasized by the treatment he received in New York and then, in 1924, at Warm Springs, in Georgia. Doctors assume, with the lack of imagination so sadly typical of the medical profession, that paralysis will have a depressing effect on the patient's ego. Consequently, they concentrate upon restoring it. Roosevelt's ego was, of course, in excellent shape even before he had the attack and in even better shape after his convalescence started. Treatment to enlarge the Roosevelt ego, though it came under the head of the coals-to-Newcastle branch of medicine, was carried on assiduously by his physicians for several years and Roosevelt responded vigorously to it. One reason why the President likes Warm Springs and feels at home there now is no doubt the fact that there not only he but all the other patients, who get the same treatment, are urged to feel superior to people who have not had paralysis—no doubt somewhat justifiably.

Nations enjoy periods of maximal artistic and commercial prosperity after victorious wars, when the surplus energy left over from the victory and a sense of release from calamity combine to produce a burst of creative power. Individuals often react in much the same way after grave illnesses. When the whole organism has made a sort of desperate war effort to repel the threat to its existence, the effort carries on through convalescence and becomes habitual. This general rule, intensified in Roosevelt's case by the special

71814

EMORY AND HENRY LIBRARY

factors noted above, also operated in his favor; and so did one other axiom.

In evaluating the special effects upon Roosevelt of his special illness, the point is usually overlooked that the most remarkable and fundamental aspect of the whole affair was that *something* happened which had *some* effect. Ordinarily, a man of thirty-eight has experienced all the major chiselings of environment that can mold his character. The statue is by then usually complete and for circumstance to go on working overtime is highly unconventional. When this occurs, the statue must inevitably be unusual; and at that age, illness is one of the few things left that can occur. Putting the cart before the horse in considering the case of his friend Gilbert Chesterton, Bernard Shaw argued that men of genius often fall ill at forty; Chesterton took a more accurate view of the matter in considering the illness that helped to remodel his hero St. Francis from a flashy poseur into a spartan saint. Before he was paralyzed, Roosevelt was a brash young man who had been insulated from reality by wealth, protection and facile success. After it, he was a wiser, much older man, who had seen life closely, although briefly, in the disguise of death.

In 1924, Al Smith invited Roosevelt to make the nominating speech at the New York convention, on the suggestion of Louis Howe, who thought the experience might be a good tonic for Roosevelt's morale. By 1928, Roosevelt's morale was not in much question; and when Smith urged him to run for governor, he accepted with reluctance caused only by his hope that with another year or two at Warm Springs, he might regain his footing entirely. The Roosevelt who ran for governor of New York in 1928 resembled the Roosevelt who had run for vice-president in 1920 as a powerful battleship resembles a fast destroyer. However, no one knew this yet, any more than Boss Murphy had known that Roosevelt amounted to anything at all in 1911. Even in 1932, so astute an observer as Walter Lippmann felt quite justified in reporting that Roosevelt was "a pleasant man who, without any important qualification for the office, would very much like to be President." Lippmann had known Roosevelt well, through World War I, in Washington; and on the ancient record Roosevelt was just as he described him.

Roosevelt's famed "Happy Warrior" speech for Smith in 1924, like so many he has uttered since, was not his own composition. Judge

Proskauer, Smith's pal, wrote it, aided by its subject. The speech, however, plus the second "Happy Warrior" address of 1928, tended to confirm the legend of solid friendship between Roosevelt and his predecessor in Albany. The legend collapsed when Roosevelt used the governorship to outdistance Smith for the Democratic nomination four years later. This was unjustly regarded as a breach of Roosevelt loyalty, like his subsequent discharge of Farley, who helped him more directly to get it.

In fact, of course, as soon as Roosevelt got to Albany it was likely that he would go on to the White House. The Depression, and a second plurality so much bigger than his first that it broke Smith's record, made Roosevelt's destination certain. As a gubernatorial executive, Roosevelt did a good job in Albany, as a campaigner for the Presidency, he did even better. Both functions coincided in the Jimmy Walker crisis of 1932, when the mayor of New York was found to be implicated in an old-school Tammany scandal. Gubernatorially, Roosevelt applied the wait-and-see-if-the-man-dies system; candidationally, he applied the wait-and-let-trouble-develop system. Like the desk-chair system, the two dovetailed perfectly. Walker did not die but he obligingly resigned at the appropriate moment, just after the crisis had got hot enough for Roosevelt to show his mastery over it, as a sort of warmup for what followed shortly afterward.

In order to understand Franklin Roosevelt it is necessary, first, to understand the country which produced him and which he purports to run.

The United States, as it exists today, is the effect of a great number of past causes. The first of these causes is the fact that America was discovered by Columbus in 1492.

At that time there were many millions of people living in Europe at a fairly high level of civilization. In North America there was no one at all, except a handful of red Indians whose paucity was such that there are more of them alive now than there were then.

The fact that the Western Hemisphere was not even found until Europe was pretty much what it is today is of profound significance. A religious person might say that Providence had sealed away half the terrestrial globe to keep until man had proved, by finding it, that he was competent to use it properly. Taking a more mundane, less optimistic view, it is as though we today were to find not only that we could reach Mars by means of a fairly simple voyage, but also that Mars was a regular garden spot, just waiting for some tenants.

If such a discovery were made, one may be sure that many people would hasten off to Mars. Similarly, quite soon after the discovery of the Western Hemisphere—an event unique in history and now quite incapable of repetition save on the astronomical plane —people began moving into it, in droves. However, even more people stayed at home; and it is worth while to note the difference between those who stayed and those who did not stay.

It is clear on the face of it that people who came to the Western Hemisphere were those who rebelled against their native environment. Some of them were criminals, whose naughty rebelliousness was what caused the native environment to throw them out. Others were law-abiding people whose rebellion was expressed solely by the fact of their departure. But the fact remains that, whatever other qualities they had in common, all had enough enterprise to be dissatisfied where they were; and to take a chance that things would be better elsewhere.

The Europeans who went to South Amer-

ica and those who came to North America encountered environments which differed in
many ways. One of the differences was that
the South American natives were sufficiently
numerous partially to absorb the newcomers
or sufficiently docile to be absorbed by them.
In North America, however, the Indians were
shy, the forests vast, and the intruders picky.
In consequence, there was no mixing of
blood. What happened instead was an experi-
ment in environmental population development comparable to no other except possibly
the Flood. Only this time, instead of having a
fresh deck of all animals in an old world, what
was provided was a fresh deck of one kind
of animals in a new world.

If any such set of astounding and utterly
novel causes as this had produced a country
exactly, or even at all, like the old countries
in Europe, it would have been a miracle indeed. Instead, what occurred was no miracle
at all; it was simply a totally new sort of
country. This is an important fact to bear in
mind; because people who try to explain the
oddities of the United States of America by
any such trivial or secondary differences as
its strategical location, its form of government or its economy are missing the point
entirely. These differences exist, it is true;

but they are only derivatives of the original differences noted above, contrived by geography and good luck or God.

When they got to North America, the swarms of purebred Europeans, criminal and otherwise, found a state of affairs which at least rewarded them in their hope of finding something new. Furthermore, it was new—and this too is a providential dispensation worth remembering—in precisely the way most gratifying to the impulses that had caused them to find it. In America, the enterprising people who had chosen to risk coming there found an environment in which enterprise and the readiness to take risks were precisely the qualities that paid off best—whereas in Europe the qualities that had paid off best had been obedience and a readiness not to take risks.

Naturally enough, a sharp misunderstanding between the people in America and those in Europe was bound to develop as soon as the passage of a few generations had dimmed the perceptions of each group. (People in one country naturally think of people in other countries as counterparts of themselves, since they have never seen any kind of people except themselves. And it is thus incredible to them that people in other countries have different sets of standards and incentives.)

Just as Americans were accustomed to enterprise and to fending for themselves both by their original aptness and their later practice, so people in England could not imagine such a state of mind. The fact that some of the ideas of the American Revolution were generated by freak, stay-at-home rebels in France or that some freak stay-at-home rebels in England sympathized with it does not alter the argument in the slightest.

After their revolution, Americans set up a form of government which, whatever else it may have been intended to do, was certainly not intended to maintain a status quo. They then set out in earnest to conquer their environment and within a hundred years or so made a good job of it.

Through all this process, one rule held: everyone was doing the best he could for himself. All Americans engaged in plain and cutthroat competition at all times. And a case could be made that America is now a peace-loving country, internationally speaking, primarily because its population has always been able to channel off its sadistic impulses in a perpetual, bloodless, personal war with each other, nationally speaking.

This would account for the fact that, except when fighting in wars, Europeans are polite and docile, whereas Americans are brusque and cantankerous. In any case, by the time of World War I Americans were a thoroughly special and highly competitive breed of person; and they would have been even more special, perhaps so special as not to be recognizable as human at all in the merely European sense, had it not been for the fact that new Europeans kept adding themselves to the original test tube, thus modifying its contents to a slight degree.

However, by the time World War I was over, with the environment conquered and the country fairly well filled up, America was more or less, socially speaking, in the same condition that European countries had been in when Columbus made his voyage. The chief difference was that Americans were not accustomed to this state of affairs, and that the spirit of enterprise and competition was just as strong as though it had still been equally appropriate.

The competitive spirit of America, deprived of an environmental outlet, turned in upon itself. People began to contend not primarily against the environment and secondarily each other, but against each other solely. Money-making, which had previously been a legitimate way of keeping score in a legitimate contest, boiled up into a vapor of abstractions like installment plans and the stock market, which had in common the fact that no real cash was involved in either one. The vapor smelled good but lacked vitamins.

What followed from this, and other causes, was of course the great Depression; and in view of the foregoing it is not hard to see why the Depression in the United States was totally different in kind as well as more severe in degree than the Depression elsewhere.

Other countries had never had occasion to believe much in intramural competitions or in money as a means of keeping score in them. Consequently, business collapse in other countries was neither quite so practically painful nor quite so spiritually shocking.

The United States, however, had always believed in everything concerned with competition, and in little else. Therefore, to discover that competition was no good and that business was a washout, and finally even that a bank was the wrong place to put one's money, was to Americans an extremely unkind cut from Brutus.

In 1928, America had eloquently expressed its ultimate faith in business, money-making and enterprise generally by putting into the White House, for the very first time, a businesslike, self-enriched engineer, the very apotheosis of American competitive virtue as it had always previously been defined.

When Herbert Hoover, one year later, proved not only quite incapable of correcting the situation but even of seeing that there was anything fundamentally wrong with it, this was the straw that almost broke the camel's back.

America had to face the fact that apparently business and everything concerned with it was worthless and also the fact that business itself didn't know what to do and even lacked the sense to see that it had to do something.

The nation was totally, and hopelessly, appalled; and it elected Franklin Roosevelt.

When Franklin Delano Roosevelt was inaugurated for the first time, on March 4, 1933, the situation was of the sort which, because it does sometimes actually occur, gives to the work of epic dramatists that verisimilitude without which they would all be hopelessly implausible and which, by inverse reasoning, then supports the notion that truth is stranger than fiction. What it did was to bring face to face, on the one hand, a man whose entire life had been spent in seeking out, wrestling against and finally defeating every sort of crisis and, on the other hand, a crisis so monstrous that it really seemed entirely beyond human mastery. Furthermore, to add the final touch of suspense to this situation, the audience, which was really more than an audience since it was itself a party to the action, was quite aware of the horrid nature of the crisis but quite unaware of the strength of its antagonist. The situation was approximately that of David and Goliath and also that of St. George and the Dragon.

Properly speaking, it was the moment for which Roosevelt had been first born and then made, and he took perfect advantage of it. First of all he seized his slingshot, in the form of a radio microphone, and delivered with it a pellet that struck the giant Depression exactly between the eyes. This pellet was his speech to the effect that all the country had to fear was fear itself. The idea was exactly suited both to the American character in general and to the American dilemma in particular. It was, also, absolutely true. In stating this idea Roosevelt was not putting forth a notion he had read somewhere in some book. Indeed, ideas of the opposite kind are furnished by detective stories, which may be why

Roosevelt finds them funny. What he was doing was giving the country the benefit of his own experience with all the crises he had encountered in his own career, from the crisis of the jumping jack to the crisis of his infantile paralysis.

Having demolished the giant, by David technique, Roosevelt proceeded to slay the Dragon, by St. George technique. This process was a shade less sudden but in its own way equally spectacular. It took the form of sly and sprightly legislative swordplay during the whole of which the Dragon was writhing, gnashing and spitting out blue, or more properly red, flames while Roosevelt hopped about in a frenzy of enthusiastic butchery, cutting off claws, ears, and occasionally a tooth which, with fine bravado, he would pop into his pocket as a souvenir.

The intense dragon-fight portion of Roosevelt's first term lasted through the first hundred days. By that time, the beast, while still unprepossessing, was clearly powerless to do much more than wriggle. Roosevelt, on the other hand, was by this time more than a mere president. He had become a national hero of almost mystical significance; and, whereas the Dragon was no longer supernatural, all Roosevelt's actions seemed to possess a kind of classic magic. He thus explained why, even in 1936, the Dragon was still wriggling; it was because he liked the fight and wanted the poor old creature—no better really than an alligator—to enjoy a breathing spell.

Roosevelt saw the country's trouble in grand and Herculean terms. On the one hand, there was big business, a mean and intolerable tyrant, which was chiefly responsible for the mess. On the other hand, there were the common people, a pitiful and helpless victim, which had to suffer for it. All the legislation which Roosevelt used to combat the Depression was based on this conception of the difficulty; and the conception was at least partially the right one. On the grand scale, everyone, including especially the Congress, agreed with it and helped Roosevelt to put it into action.

Roosevelt began, quite properly, with money. First, by his handling of the bank panic he made clear that money as such would continue to exist. Then, by means of the PWA and the WPA, he made it clear that there would be more available, especially for those who had the least of it. Whether these schemes were economically sound is not, here, material—unless one considers that economy is so profound an expression of the human psyche that its laws correspond with the apparently unrelated laws of morality and ethics. Emotionally, they were entirely sound, both as expressions of Roosevelt's character and as impressions on the national character, and in effecting them Roosevelt was indubitably and confessedly acting on an emotional rather than a calculating basis.

The money tutors whom Roosevelt employed at the time assured him that, by letting funds seep into the social sugar lump at the bottom, not only the lower strata but the whole lump would absorb the funds by a sort of capillary attraction. The President was much pleased by their theories and never seemed in the least disposed to assemble tutors of the opposite school, who might have suggested pouring the new money in at the top. However, he did not really understand the reasoning of the economists or think that he should try to do so. Instead, he said frankly that he would try different methods and discard the ones that didn't work. On this basis, he slapped vast taxes on inheritance, whacked at corporations' surplus profits, and tinkered with the dollar.

Roosevelt's own interest in money, which at best had never been acute, began gradually to develop now that money was a weapon in his battles for the underdog, against their wicked bosses. He showed this interest in a characteristic way. Roosevelt dealt with huge sums of money through his underlings but these deals were abstractions and left him somewhat puzzled. He could not understand, for instance, why the rising price level— which should have resulted in increased purchasing power, which should have raised the price level further—suddenly leveled out about 1935. He really came to grips with money in another way entirely, not through the devaluation of the dollar, but through diminishing the size of the dollar bill, which was in itself an even more symbolic act. One day Henry Morgenthau presented Roosevelt with a blueprint for the new bill. Roosevelt, who likes to design new stamps and anything else he can get his hands on, scrutinized it joyfully until his eye fell on a little insignificant design on the left, put in to balance the significant Great Seal of the United States on the right. "Why not use the reverse of the Great Seal here instead?" the President inquired. What the reverse side of the Great Seal was, his aides presently found out. It shows a pyramid and a mystic eye, both surmounted by the motto *Novus Ordo Seclorum*; in Roosevelt English, a complete New Deal.

The *Novus Ordo Seclorum* which the President proposed to effect and to a large degree did effect, was defined by himself in a famous speech which he made before the Commonwealth Club of San Francisco during the 1932 campaign. In this speech the general thesis laid down was in effect that, whereas during the period of United States geographical and industrial expansion the moral disadvantages of piratical competition had been outweighed by the practical advantages accruing from it, that period had now ended; and henceforth, if the United States were to run properly, piracy would have to be stamped out and competition controlled by a beneficent federal government. With this attitude most sane people heartily concurred. It was not until later that the country learned exactly what he had in mind. In stopping the piracy, the President was not altogether adverse to stopping the competition along with it, which amounted to chopping down the tree to get the cherries.

There is no necessity to examine here the individual schemes by which the President proceeded to implement his program. All of them were set up along agency lines and run by underlings, directly responsible to the executive branch of the government. All of them purported to benefit the common people as distinguished from their overlords. And most of them were more or less maladministered, as was inevitable for reasons previously set forth. However, with the sad exception of the NRA, most of the maladministration scarcely had time to become apparent before the end of the President's first term.

The only really obvious defeat in Roosevelt's first term was the fact that he broke his campaign promise to cut down government expenses and, instead, ran them up to totals previously undreamed of. However, in breaking a campaign promise Roosevelt had excellent precedents and moral justification. In politics all officeholders are permitted by general convention to break their campaign promises, and invariably do so. This does not mean that all politicians are dishonest but merely that honesty in politics, like honesty among thieves, is channeled in a special direction. A more true defect was that the President also began to disregard his promises to his associates. This politicians are forbidden to do by political convention; but it too did not became apparent until much later.

There was one more serious defect in

Roosevelt's first term. This was that, when it might still have been possible to do something about the impending war in Europe, he ignominiously failed to do it. However, this did not become apparent until much, much later; and, as it was a defect of omission rather than commission, it is really impossible to say how much he was to blame. And to balance this, his dams and what-not came in handy when the war began.

The truth is that, looking back on it in nostalgic mood, Roosevelt's first term was a howling success. Little Sistie and Buzzie Dall scampered about the White House, and Mrs. Roosevelt, not yet a daily essayist, scampered about the country taking people's minds off more serious troubles. Dashboard radios and four-wheel brakes improved motoring conditions. The national novelties were skiing, swing bands, Huey Long, and pinball. Rummy was a children's game, the Prince of Wales had not met Wallis Simpson, and Margaret Mitchell was still sharpening her pencils. Willkie, at this period, was just settling into his stride as president of Commonwealth and Southern, and Tom Dewey was a chore boy for LaGuardia, who was just beginning his career as Mayor of New York. In France someone named a wharf on the Seine the

"Quai Franklin Roosevelt," where huge ship-
ments of red and white wine were stored waiting for him to repeal the Volstead Act; and in
1936, with business getting better daily, an
obscure, earnest Kansas governor named
Alfred Landon earned a modest niche in history by carrying Vermont and Maine in the
worst defeat ever suffered in a presidential
election.

Swept into office on a vast wave of confidence and approval by a convalescent country,
the President on January 20, 1937 began a
second term, which was almost as sensationally
disappointing as the first had been the opposite and for exactly the same reasons.

Roosevelt, in his second term, was handicapped by the fact that it came after the first
one. The handicap was both objective and
subjective in almost equal parts.

Objectively, Roosevelt had been in an excellent position at the outset of his first term.
To have an untried captain take the helm in
the midst of a tempest had naturally presented
itself to the country, in its excited state, as
an appalling risk, but necessary since the only
apparent alternative was shipwreck. Consequently, when the captain had first an-

nounced that he could not only steer the boat
but also make the waves stop rolling, and
then had proceeded to make good his boast, it
seemed miraculous to everyone. To Roosevelt
himself it did not seem miraculous at all; and
this made the magic all the more enchanting.
However, like all enchantments, it was only
temporary. This was because the idea con-
veyed to most people—for whom, unlike
Franklin Roosevelt, a crisis is an impediment,
not a stimulus—was that, if Roosevelt could
do that well in a storm, he could do anything
at all in favorable weather. At the beginning
of Roosevelt's second term, the weather was
reasonably favorable; and now, far from being
an untried captain, the President was a
seasoned helmsman whose comparatively easy
job was just to get the ship to port on
schedule.

Subjectively, the new situation also worked
against the President. One of the defects of
people who are encouraged by crises is that
they are discouraged by anticlimaxes; and
Roosevelt's second term was a double anticlimax. It was an anticlimax, first, because he
had dealt with the original crisis so effectively
that it was long gone by the time he was
inaugurated for the second time. Having performed an impossible miracle under stress

when no one thought he could do it, he now found that a second miracle in the midst of comparative calm, when it could not be performed, was definitely expected of him. Second, it was an anticlimax because by this time people were actually beginning to find flaws in the earlier miracle. Thus, whereas in the first campaign Roosevelt had been in the happy position of a person who could make promises to a country that wanted to hear them, in the second campaign he was in the less favorable position of a man who has to call attention to his payments on the promises which, in the nature of things, had not been universally satisfactory. Instead of a ringing and classic combination of profound philosophical truth and altruistic common sense, like his banishment of fear, all he had to offer was the tinny self-congratulation "we planned it that way." And this sounded even flatter when (a) the plans went awry in the 1937 "recession" and (b) the Supreme Court presumed to say that, quite aside from their impracticality as shown by the recession, the plans had been illegal in the first place.

The recession was something Roosevelt could deal with very well, because it came from beneath. He coined a phrase about "economic royalists" and let it go at that.

The Supreme Court's attitude, on the other hand, naturally set his teeth on edge. Roosevelt's efforts to make the Supreme Court amenable to his wishes—which was, in effect, what the fight boiled down to—consequently turned out to be a most revealing squabble. It gave the country a new insight into his character and changed his relations with it deeply and incorrigibly.

The Roosevelt point of view is not hard to decipher. Throughout his career he had rarely encountered real authority; when he had encountered it—in the form of snobbism, bossism, Hooverism and Entrenched Wealth —two things had characterized the encounter. One was that the authority was villainous, in the popular mythology; the other was that Roosevelt had triumphed over it. From this reasoning, Roosevelt—deluded perhaps by his own self-assurance—had subconsciously fallen into two errors of logic both as absurd as the conclusion that because all horses are animals all animals are horses. He had come to assume that, since the authority he had previously encountered was regarded as villainous, all authority which he encountered would be considered villainous; and that, since he had always triumphed over authority, he would continue to do so. Perhaps the basis

for the rash assumption in Roosevelt's subconscious reasoning was that he felt he had to
triumph over all authority. In any case,
ordinarily acutely conscious of the effect he
is making on people, whether individually or
en masse, the President was on this occasion
so completely in error about the effect that he
resembled an actor playing Hamlet in the
costume of a clown. Throughout the fight, he
took the attitude not only that he was in a
heroic role but that everyone else would
recognize him in it. Instead, everyone recognized his role as that of a spoiled brat, which
increased his sense of aggrievement.

The reason why so few people saw Roosevelt as he saw himself in this particular
episode is entirely clear. For most human
beings, some of the reverence that stems from
the father-relationship in infancy is projected
toward public institutions in adult life. In
England, this reverence is concentrated upon
the crown; among South African natives it
may be directed toward witch doctors; in the
United States it is split up among several
recipients of which the Supreme Court, de-
servedly or not, is one. Consequently, for exactly the same reasons that people had ap-
plauded Roosevelt's attacks on usurping or
discarded authority symbols, they deplored

this attack on a more ultimate authority symbol which to them was still entirely satisfactory. And the fact that Roosevelt, to whom alone the symbol was objectionable, himself completely misunderstood his role in this respect made him look not only impudent but silly.

The exciting thing about the Supreme Court fight was that, though for utterly different reasons, it was just as important to the country, which by and large backed the court, as it was to Roosevelt, who was determined to take it apart. But beyond sensing the semireligious importance of the contest to themselves, people sensed its profound personal importance to the President, and the contest thus developed into a far more important one than the issues at stake had ever warranted. The battle yelps of the procourt faction were, of course, that it was unfair to change the rules or the umpire in the middle of the game; and the countercry was that the court was not an umpire and had no right to make the rules. Of the two, the latter was perhaps more logical; but logicality was not a relevant factor.

Had the President been guided by logic in the court fight, he would never have got into it. It was obvious from the outset that the practical, as distinguished from the symbolic, results he might have gained by victory he was sure to gain anyway by the passage of time. Presently, through the passage of time, he did indeed gain them; but by then he had abdicated from the incalculable, superhuman prestige which he had previously enjoyed. The electorate had now discovered that the wizard who could vanquish panic with a phrase was really just an ordinary human being who could not only lose a decision to a higher power but also lose his temper over losing it. This was an extremely salutary discovery for all concerned, because it put the relations of Roosevelt and the country on a realistic footing and ended any chance that he would engender, whether for his own profit or that of some successor, that filial reverence toward a mere head of state of which the total absence is essential to democracy.

The fight against the Supreme Court, in which Roosevelt was thus fundamentally the loser, was motivated on his part by exactly the same impulses that had motivated his fight against Big Business, which he had won. But having won his fight against business apropos of the Depression, Roosevelt made a great error in perpetuating the fight over the recession. And this error had to do with his feeling about money. Lack of interest in and true understanding of money was what had chiefly encouraged the President to pump such vast quantities of it into the bottom of the economy to considerable advantage in his first term, when everybody was dirt poor. The same lack of interest in it caused him to mishandle a much more subtle state of affairs which developed in his second term when the condition was not that nobody had any money, but just that they wanted more. This time, instead of working out to his advantage, Roosevelt's cavalier attitude toward the currency worked out the other way.

Roosevelt's legislation on behalf of the common people—as represented by laborers, farmers, unemployed, the indigent aged, CCC boys and the rest—had certainly improved their economic situation to some degree, and benefited them to that extent. However, it seems quite debatable whether this is the maximum benefit that it is possible to confer upon common people; and this is because of what they are. Indeed, the essential point about common people generally, and those of the United States especially, is not that they are common but that they are capable of becoming uncommon. And the idea that all people are created equal is realistic primarily because it implies that, after being created, they are not equal at all. In other words, the idea of competition is implicit in, if not the very object of, the whole American system; and it is out of a desire not to end competition but to increase it by making it as fair, and therefore as lively, as possible that we insist quite properly that the horses start off together at the beginning of the race. This, obviously, is exactly the reverse of saying that the horses must still be lined up together when they trot past the wire at the finish, for in that case they are engaged in a parade and not a race. And it was precisely to avoid all such parades, and not to engage in them, that the population came to America and stayed here in the first place.

Much the same sort of metaphor may be applied to the common people's overlords, financial and otherwise. These individuals feel, justifiably or otherwise, that they have run the race and finished well up forward. Consequently, they consider themselves entitled to certain prizes and are condonably chagrined when the prizes are withdrawn from them.

Of course, the metaphor of a horse race is not entirely applicable to human affairs; and it is undoubtedly true, in any case, that much of Roosevelt's legislation has tended to equalize the starting position of the field and thus improved the sporting quality of the event. However, it is equally true that in none of his legislation, either that of a punitive or that of a charitable inspiration, has there been much indication that this was the purpose, or even that he regards human life as a race in which the best prizes should go to the best runners. In this he has been as much out of sympathy with the common people as he has been with economic royalists. The rich, after all, would still have their interior feeling of self-satisfaction even if all their prizes were confiscated; whereas, deprived of a chance to compete both against the rich and with each other to the best of their abilities, the common people would have absolutely nothing.

Roosevelt's failure to assign any major place, let alone a primary place, to the universal and entirely primary human desire to compete—using the word for its exact English, not its abstruse Marxist, meaning—can also be studied on the graph lines of his career. He himself, as a small child, had no little brothers to compete with; he did not acquire much relish for the habit of competitive sports at school or college; and his later competition, in the area of politics, was for such special and abstract rewards that it would have been surprising indeed if he had ever recognized it as such, let alone identified it with the vulgar competitive drives of the common people.

What ordinary people compete for is nothing so grand or so remote as power, prestige or influence. It is simply money. Money is certainly important to people as a means of buying bread and butter and a roof; but it is much more important to them for entirely different reasons, as a currency based on, and standing for, the gold of independent action. In the world of human illusion, money is the method whereby most people, and especially most Americans, keep score, measure their progress, and base their self-esteem. They thus give it a value out of all relation to its practical efficacy; but no one who fails to understand this relish, and the reasons for it, can really hope to understand them.

Roosevelt's failure to understand about money is betokened by his apparent notion that he can really hurt rich people by taking it away from them or deeply benefit poor ones by giving it to them; because to any decent American earned money is primarily important, like the cup one gets for winning a race, as a token of superiority, whereas money

conferred gratuitously is merely counterfeit.
Nor is it hard to perceive why Roosevelt fails
to understand it. The reason is simply that he
has never had to study it. Under this handicap, no one else would understand about it
either.

In Mrs. Roosevelt's biography of her son,
she remarks, honestly enough, that Franklin
was never given an allowance because there
was no place for him to spend it and because
he had everything he needed anyway. For a
person who has everything that money can
buy, it would naturally seem absurd to struggle to acquire it. Consequently, on leaving
college, as has been previously noted, Roosevelt was entirely at a loose end until he found
something worth competing for—prestige
and attention. His own discovery of these as
superior prizes in the race inevitably gave him
a feeling of disdain for those who would compete for money, something he already had.
But in disdaining winners in the race for
money, Roosevelt had quite pardonably
failed to perceive that those who were losers
—none of whom he met in Wall Street—were
in the race at all. It may never have occurred
to Roosevelt that poor people really want not
so much a better house, or more food, or a
new suit as, much more fundamentally, the

power to choose which one of these or many other things they want; and the assurance furthermore that this great power lies within themselves. Most people can acquire this kind of security only by earning money; and that is what security means, and why plain money is important.

By the end of Roosevelt's second term, the weakness of his policy toward the Supreme Court and toward the American eagerness to compete for money, combined with his deficiencies as an administrator, although they derived from the same causes as his popular conquest of the Depression and chastisement of business in his first term, had made up a strong case against him. What with the general American prejudice against reverence for a head of state, this case would probably have been quite adequate to put Roosevelt out of office in the campaign of 1940 had it been ably stated. Furthermore, it looked as though it might be ably stated, in case Roosevelt ran again, since the counsel-for-defense of private enterprise was none other than the Roosevelt *bête blanche*, Mr. Wendell Willkie, who had the indictment down letter perfect. Willkie, however, did not get a chance to address the jury on the subject for, ironically, the same reason that made the stating of it relevant, because it permitted Roosevelt to run for his third term. That was the war in Europe.

In addition to dwarfing the problem of Roosevelt's mismanagement and misunderstanding of his function, the war was the grandest crisis in the whole of human history. And Roosevelt reacted characteristically.

# IV

$I$N 1936, Hitler consulted the stars and marched into the Rhineland. France turned to England for help in throwing him out. England thought over all the elements in the situation, including the United States, and replied, "No dice." It was at this point that England made a great, and inexcusable, error. Before that, to slap Hitler down would have been meddlesome and unjustifiable. After that, it was justifiable but difficult. The march into the Rhineland was the exact place where, it appears in retrospect, the action should have been, and was not, taken.

Suppose for the sake of argument, that the process of buck-passing summarized above had been arrested and reversed by positive action in the United States. If, instead of watching the whole affair from a balcony seat, the United States had stepped onto the stage, as it was later obliged to do, and had said in effect to the British, "This is the time to deal with Hitler. If you help France now, we will help you both. But if you don't both get busy now, you will have to take the consequences."

The result of such a course might well have been that Hitler would have gone into the history books as a clownish bluffer, and that World War II would have been avoided. Of course, all these are the thoughts of a Monday morning quarterback. Possibly, even if the above diagnosis is correct, the world, which would not have known the trouble it had been spared, would have developed an even more credulous attitude toward Germany than it showed at the time and an even worse war would have developed later. Nonetheless, it is an interesting line of speculation; and we may follow it along for a moment.

When confronted as to why, if it saw the war coming all along, as it claims to have done, and indeed should have done, it did nothing to prevent it, the Roosevelt administration has a stock answer. The answer is that, although it did foresee the war, the people didn't and were therefore not disposed to back up their government in backing England to back France. The sound track then runs as follows: QUESTION: If the Administration wanted the people to know that Hitler was a real devil, why didn't it take the pains to tell them? ANSWER: It did tell them, but the people did not believe it.

This reply is not a good one. As late as 1937 the people were in a mood to believe anything the President told them. As early as 1933, a business boom based on war production would have been much more apropos than it was in 1942; and a war production program then, in addition to being much better business than the WPA, would have made the war itself superfluous.

What it comes down to is that either the Administration did not foresee the war, which, in view of its information sources, would be a shocking symptom of myopia, or else it did foresee the war but performed a remarkably poor job of calling attention to the matter, intentionally or otherwise. The latter diagnosis seems to fit the facts better than the former, though both are applicable. What seems to have happened was simply that the war was foreseen, but not quite so clearly or so soon as it should have been; and that, when it was foreseen, there was not much disposition to call attention to the tardy discovery—partly because of the very fact that, since it was already too late to get the situation under complete control, the tardiness was the essential point rather than the discovery. In 1933, the President's speechmaking assistants used to regard his brief allusions to foreign affairs as a waste of valuable radio time which might have been devoted to domestic problems; by 1938, such allusions were indeed worse than a waste of time, since there was not much to be said except that, owing to our bad management as much as anybody else's, we would eventually be obliged to fight the war that we had won a generation earlier.

To excuse Roosevelt's undoubted failure to sell the prospect of war to the United States as soon as he should have done on the ground that the heads of state of England and France, who had even better reason for doing so, failed even more miserably is really somewhat difficult. The fact is that France was a political mess, not capable of buying any idea, let alone an important one; and Chamberlain had no idea to sell, and couldn't have sold one if he had.

Equally implausible is the excuse that Roosevelt did try to sell the prospect in his famous Chicago "quarantine" speech in 1937.

By this time, the war was already inevitable; and by snarling at the Supreme Court, while ignoring Hitler, Roosevelt had already put himself in the position of the boy who shouted "wolf" before the real wolf chased him.

In truth, Roosevelt was a past master in selling the United States public anything, and, before 1937, the public was in a buying mood. Consequently, the most charitable excuse in Roosevelt's case is that, conditioned to people as he was, he simply did not find it possible to accept the logical hypothesis that other people were conditioned so differently as Messrs. Hitler and Mussolini. Certainly his attitude toward these potentates in the preshooting stages showed a touching and likeable faith in the peacefulness of human nature, which nothing in the behavior of the recipients had ever warranted; and his attitude toward the Japanese, even up to the moment of Pearl Harbor, did much more credit to his heart than to his head.

Of course, once the crisis was at hand, the President showed courageous common sense and grand-scale ingenuity not only in handling it but in turning it to his advantage. The over-all political decision that we could not let England lose was courageous common sense; the practical scheme for expressing this decision by means of lend-lease was ingenious. In turning the crisis to his own advantage the importance of the factors was reversed. When, in the 1940 campaign, the President promised the country again and again and again that "we will not participate in foreign wars and will not send our army, navy, or air forces to fight in foreign lands," he knew very well that the audience would not catch the double-meaning. And it was almost devious to pretend by implication later on that the very ambiguity of the word "foreign" proved the artless sincerity of his conviction that the war in Europe was not "foreign" but our own. This issue, in any case, was not basically decisive. What decided the election was that in 1940, as distinguished from 1932, everyone knew that Roosevelt was a good skipper in a storm; and in 1940, as distinguished from 1936, the storm was certainly rising. The obvious conclusion was to let Roosevelt ride it out.

As a war president, Roosevelt must be judged by his conduct of the war, that is, the decisions he has taken that affect it. Roughly speaking, the decisions fall into two main categories, big and little. The big decisions concern over-all strategy and objectives. The little decisions, owing to the way the President runs things, come down chiefly to his choice of personnel. So far, judged by results, both big and little decisions have been good on balance, with some notable exceptions.

The big decisions have so far been three: (1) to beat Germany first and Japan second; (2) to demand unconditional surrender, that is, keep the peace terms secret from the enemy; and (3) to fight a slow, concentric war, instead of a rapid, straight-line one. The first decision, like the previous one to send supplies to England, was correct but not especially brilliant. The only alternative was to defeat Japan first and Germany second and this was obviously less practical as well as less desirable. The second decision, too, though not so clearly obligatory, was dictated by events rather than selected by Roosevelt; and it is still subject to some modifications. As to the third decision, judgment must be postponed, but here at least Roosevelt had more other lines to choose from, and picked the one he followed chiefly on his own hook. The North African campaign, as first step in a roundabout process of squeezing Germany in the steel ring she had yelped about

so prematurely was a Roosevelt tactic.
Whether or not it works out better than a
quick jab at the heart will be more apparent
when the steel ring is completed.

In selecting people to run the war for him,
Roosevelt has, by and large, had two big
groups to deal with: civilians, to run the
civilian part of the war, and servicemen, to
run the services. This has been advantageous
as compared with his previous situation,
where he picked only civilians. The services,
by definition, exclude from the field of choice
the worst type to which the President is partial—jolly talkers. In the Army, Navy and
Air Force, promotions may be slow, but they
are made competitively, on the merit-and-
seniority basis. Some good men may fail to
get ahead and some mediocre ones may do
so, but by and large all officers are competing violently for higher rank at all times,
and by and large the best ones get it. This
ensures that there be a reasonably full barrel
of seasoned, competent officers somewhere
near the top; and that there will not be, anywhere near the top, a swarm of loud-
mouthed, loutish juveniles, neurotic, namby-
pamby fixers, freak, five-cent philosophers,
woozy, double-talk idea-men, or little leftist
Caesars. Thus, even if Roosevelt should feel

inclined to use the same yardstick for his military advisers that he sometimes uses for civilians, it would be hard for him to do so.

So far there have been no signs that he had any wish to do so. The President did make one sensationally bad pick in the case of the admiral who was running Pearl Harbor in December, 1941. Furthermore, this pick was apparently made strictly on his own hunch, and in line with his performance-chart. The admiral in question loudly indicated an optimistic attitude toward licking Japan in a war, unlike some of his less cheery colleagues. This line of talk appealed to Roosevelt, who jumped the admiral over many of his seniors to ironically bad advantage when the optimism needed justifying. However, even the admiral in question was by no means wholly responsible for Pearl Harbor; and even he had a good record for much more than conversation.

Pearl Harbor was a grave moral shock, as well as a grave military defeat, for the United States. The job of Hawaii was not only to fight battles but also, and much more particularly, to give the alarm and to stay on guard so that the whole nation would not have to. It was thus an instance not of a soldier merely, but rather of a sentry caught

asleep on duty. To the President the shock
was especially dreadful. For one thing, he
knew the worst of the news immediately, unlike his fellow citizens who had to wait a
year. For another, it concerned particularly
his favorite branch of the service, as represented by an admiral of his own selection.
Less as a crisis than a scandal, Pearl Harbor
depressed the President, but it seems to have
had a salutary influence. Certainly, none of
his other major naval and military admin-
istrators—Marshall, King, Leahy, Eisen-
hower, Nimitz and MacArthur—have proved
less than technically excellent.

Whereas the way the President has functioned as commander in chief cannot be
discussed because the details are still mostly
military secrets, the way he has functioned
as President of the United States at war need
not be, since the details are available in the
news. By and large, however, it seems that
the President is still friendly, but a bad administrator; and that, in addition to enjoy-
ing big crises, he likes little ones. Arranging
little crises is a simple matter for him; by
appointing two of his underlings to do jobs
with overlapping fields of influence, he can
be sure a quarrel will develop. Since most of
the underlings are violently articulate, their

quarrel will be raucous. However, although the Office of War Information may be a mess, the Office of Price Administration a nuisance, the War Production Board a controversial appendage and Washington a madhouse, the fact remains that the United States power potential, as realized since 1940, has exceeded all the boldest hopes of everyone including Roosevelt, who most certainly should have some of the credit.

That the President, with equal certainty, should not get quite all the credit is due to an ironic factor overlooked in many estimates of the United States war effort. This factor —ironic because, although derided by the President at all times, it is the very same one that made his first term so successful—is the American enthusiasm for competing, in such simple terms as money. To a leftist dreamer or a world-saving idealist, it no doubt seems dreadful to suppose that, while Americans are dying in Europe or the Pacific, other Americans at home should be concerned with profits. That, nonetheless, is the way both Americans, and all the other peoples in the world, are constructed. It is ridiculous to deny that the profit motive, operating on a huger scale than it has ever operated before, and on all levels from labor to top management, has played a vast part in the American war effort. Nor is it less ridiculous to suggest that it should be otherwise. The soldiers will get their share of the benefits on returning; and if some home-front profits were exorbitant, the greedy profiteers can be jailed when the time comes to attend to it.

Of course, the war has had some compensations for the President also. In addition to being exciting in itself, it has enabled him to travel and to see new people. Furthermore, the new people have been of a new kind. Whereas all the people he met during his first ten years in Washington were his inferiors in station, the ones he hobnobs with in Quebec, Cairo and Teheran are nominally, and maybe more than nominally, equals.

The President, for example, greatly enjoyed his trip to Teheran. Prettyman, as senior valet, had the privileges of both packing and accompanying his boss. Accustomed to such jobs, he waited till the morning of departure to begin the former and knew just what to put in the bags: clothes for all types of weather, a sweater or two for the sea voyage and the knickknacks for the President's pals. Among the latter were two eight-inch silver frames, each with a presidential seal on top, containing photographs of F. D. Roosevelt. These, ordered by Grace Tully, are standard presidential gifts to bigwigs. One went to Stalin and one went to President Inonu of Turkey, because, when he got to Cairo, the President remembered that Chiang Kai-shek's wife had one already and a duplicate would only clutter up their house. The President forgot that Winston's birthday would come up during the visit and had to get him a Persian dish of some sort at the last minute. Winston, on the other hand, did much better than the President for Stalin, by taking him the famous, made-to-order Stalingrad sword, instead of just his picture.

The sea voyage, to a North African port, was pleasant. The party drank special Washington water, got cigarettes from the ship PX and ate good Army food, cooked by six Filipino boys from the presidential yacht *Potomac*. The President had the captain's quarters, with a private sun-deck. He passed his mystery stories around, had a daily massage from Commander Fox, watched his aides' gin rummy, and swapped funny stories. One of Roosevelt's favorite stories is the old one about the man who, on losing his sight and hearing, visited his doctor to see what was the matter. The doctor told his patient that he could retain his faculties if he would only stop drinking. Six months later, the doctor passed the man on the street and asked him if he had followed this advice.

"No, doctor," the man replied. "After the things I'd been hearin and seein I decided I wouldn't be missing much, so I'd rather drink."

Another story Roosevelt likes is one about a hillbilly who, after courting a girl for a year, finally found himself confronted by her father. Said the father:

"You've been calling on my daughter for a year, now, and I would like to ask you— are your intentions honorable or dishonorable?"

"You mean I get a choice?" replied the hillbilly.

From the North African port, the President flew to Cairo in an Army C-54. Backs were removed from two seats so that a rubber mattress, surrounded by a green curtain like that of a Pullman berth, could be put down. The President's twenty-six aides slept sitting. The plane flew low over the Tunisian battlefields and the route of Rommel's rout in Libya, and arrived in Cairo on Sunday afternoon, November 21. There elaborate preparations for the President's visit—first planned by himself and Churchill at Quebec in the previous August—had been carefully made by Roosevelt's Middle East deputy, General Patrick Hurley. The President stayed in a boxlike villa which is one of the four houses maintained by the United States minister to Egypt and four other countries, Alexander Kirk, who wears gray suits, shoes, ties, and buttons. The Kirk house is six miles out of Cairo, on the road toward the Pyramids. Roosevelt, who had never seen Cairo, wanted to drive in for a look but secret-service men forbade this. They said Churchill could go, because, if someone took a pot shot, he could jump and run, but the President was not mobile. Roosevelt was displeased, but obedient.

Churchill stayed at Minister of State Casey's cozy wood-surrounded villa two miles farther from the town, across the Pyramids highway. Chiang stayed in a near-by guesthouse. Mena house, the old-fashioned resort hotel across the road from the Pyramids, was where the conferences were supposed to have been held. It was actually full of generals, admirals, aides and secretaries. Most of the major talks were held from three to seven every afternoon, in Kirk's living room, where the President sat on the sofa. Madame Chiang was the interpreter. The British, who were hosts at the conference, took over thirty-four Cairo villas for the party and spent £6,500 for rent alone, not counting bar bills, food and entertainment. Cairo itself was not much disturbed by its visitors. Egyptians rode their donkeys past the Kirk house without even wondering what was happening inside. Farmers, using antique water wheels, drew water from their wells within sight of the President's bedroom window.

One of the problems of the trip was what to do about signing presidential papers. An Army courier plane went daily to and from Washington but the President was worried about the Commodity Credit Bill, which he knew would come up in his absence and which he feared might become law unless he vetoed it within the ten-day limit. Judge Rosenman studied precedents and rulings. He found that during Wilson's stay in France, papers sent by ship had taken as long as two months for the round trip. Attorney General Biddle ruled that the ten-day period started only when the President received a bill, which simplified the matter. The President, while in Cairo, spent one hour on domestic business every morning and signed twenty-five bills, including the father-draft act. His entourage ribbed the chief executive about being a fugitive from a process server and getting out of the country to duck having papers served on him. The President enjoyed the complications and one night remarked, "Well, I guess I'm the first president in history to sign a bill in Cairo, Egypt."

"Is it legal, do you think?" one of his aides inquired.

"Oh, I guess it'll have to go through the Supreme Court," the President retorted.

Next day, Minister Kirk paid a call on Egypt's premier and reported, "Nahas Pasha was most interested to hear you made a United States law in Cairo."

"You should have waited till today," the President said, "You could have told him I just vetoed four." In fact, the only bill the President vetoed in Cairo was the one to make Pearl Harbor day a holiday.

In Teheran, in addition to the bowl for Churchill, the President did some Christmas shopping, advised by Dr. Wilbur of the New York Metropolitan Museum, who happened to be there on other business. He bought hand-painted bracelets for his daughters-in-law, but what he got for Eleanor was a secret.

These trinkets were delivered to Stalin's embassy, where he stayed, by messenger from the Army PX.

With Chiang, the talks were mostly business. Stalin proved a jollier type and the President got on well with him, and better than Stalin got on with Churchill. At one time Stalin grunted to the latter, "In the last war, you said you'd fight anybody, anytime, anyplace. Now you don't want to fight anybody, anytime, anywhere." At another, the Russian dictator—whose young interpreter can take English talk in Russian shorthand and vice versa—proposed a toast to the effect that after the war the best thing to do for future peace would be to slaughter fifty thousand Prussian officers. This was a characteristic Stalin joke and Churchill failed to find it funny. Roosevelt saved the situation by remarking, "I propose an amendment to that toast. Let's settle, say, for forty-nine."

The president flew back to North Africa and returned to Washington by sea. On the morning of his arrival, reporters found him dressed in a weird plaid shirt that looked like something borrowed in Camp Carefree. Roosevelt told them about a plot to assassinate him, uncovered by the OGPU, which sounded fairly probable. Two other close squeaks had occurred but these he did not mention. One was when German bombers sank two ships at Oran the day before his unarmed plane put down there. Another was the German raid on Bari, which destroyed supply ships in the harbor. The President had been urging his party to let him stop off at Bari for a weekend.

In the best of health throughout his journey, unlike Churchill, the President caught grippe as soon as he got home again. When he catches cold, the President likes to go to bed immediately. He is an amenable invalid, perhaps because he has had lots of practice. While in bed he gets out his stamp albums and sees to putting new stamps in. For this purpose, he has a little sponge which spares him the necessity of licking. As a stamp collector, Roosevelt is better than the late King George V, but still only mediocre. He gets his best ones from friends but also puts in bids with Max Ohlman. Roosevelt's stamp collecting, in addition to being a substitute for money-collecting, is an expression of his interest in geography, which in turn is associated with his love for people, travel and excitement. Even at Groton, Roosevelt enjoyed memorizing names of distant capitals and rivers. He still finds his knack in this direction handy and has a few pet lists with which he likes to dazzle uninitiated callers. Some years ago, Joseph Kennedy, now a brushee, was amazed when the President, in chatting about a proposed transcontinental highway, reflectively and in a casual tone began to name counties it would run through, until he had named all of them.

In addition to enabling him to display erudition, the President's knowledge about such minutiae is a function of his well-developed belief in direct administration, whether the matter on hand is the global war or a window in his Warm Springs cottage. Some years ago he was discussing the latter subject with his architect, Henry Toombs, who had just brought in the final drawings. "That arch over the window," the President said. "You've never seen that in a Dutch house." Toombs argued and said finally, "Mr. Roosevelt, I've made quite a study of Dutch architecture and I know what I'm talking about."

"Where did you study Dutch architecture?"

"Pennsylvania."

Roosevelt was delighted. "You'll be interested to learn, Henry," he remarked quite rightly, "that Pennsylvania Dutch is not Dutch. It is German."

Mild arguments of this sort please Roosevelt but he insists that people who disagree with him do so politely. Some years ago, during his brief period of law practice, Roosevelt had occasion to listen at an insurance commission meeting to a rude argument from a Jewish lawyer who reviled him and the methods of the company he represented. Roosevelt grew white with anger but waited till his adversary finished. Then he leaned forward and said bitingly, "If a man is not born with manners he can acquire them."

One of the things Roosevelt likes about Jews nowadays is the fact that, in addition to being good talkers and sympathetic, the ones he has around are mostly gentle and receptive. Roosevelt's special interest in Jews dates roughly from the period of his illness and may be connected with it, in that the Jewish racial trauma and his own physical incapacity provide a common bond. Some such sense of identification with and responsibility for the weak, the wronged and the unhappy, always present in Roosevelt and fortified, along with many other elements in his character, by its unique development in early middle age, certainly lies close to the heart of his political instinct.

As a politician, Roosevelt's technical adroitness is vastly overadvertised. His weaknesses and virtues were well-illustrated by last winter's row with Congress, which stemmed from a wretchedly sarcastic and politically inept statement of a true bill of goods in his tax bill veto message. Any good professional politician, with the lifetime habit of guarding his stake in the game, would have known the message would bounce back at him. Roosevelt didn't either know or care. His only adroitness in the matter was displayed when it turned into a crisis. Then, informed that Barkley would be re-elected Senate leader, Roosevelt turned this slap at him to his own advantage by his gently phrased telegram whereby, when Barkley was re-elected, this seemed to be a tribute to the President rather than a snub.

Roosevelt's very lack of true technical dexterity often gives the appearance of superhuman cunning, just as his radio fireside chats, hailed as masterpieces of suave, calculated oratory, are in fact just an expression of his belief in direct executive methods on a national scale. The radio has rendered representational democracy obsolete by putting the whole nation, if not the whole world, on the same intimate footing with its leaders as that enjoyed by the citizens of minute Greek city-states. Roosevelt, whose presidential career luckily coincided with the decade in which radio attained this enormously significant increase in stature, was better equipped than any of his contemporaries, both among heads of state and among local rivals, to capitalize on it. The President's radio popularity seems to cut both ways, however. One school of thought believes that it gives him an unfair advantage over all opponents. According to this theory, it takes years to build up a top-rank Crossley rating and it is hopeless to expect a rival attraction to outpull the President on the air in view of his twelve-year head-start. The other school of thought points out that no show can run forever and that the President's pulling power has been falling off. Indeed, recent checkups seem to show that many listeners nowadays like his friendly Groton hum for the first ten minutes and then just switch over to some mind reader or a dance band.

No reader, however indulgent, should really be expected to accept, on the face of it, an author's argument that, just because so much has been said on his subject, it is advisable not to let the matter drop, but to say more. Instead, he should want to know, first, why previous writings have caused so much confusion and, second, what, precisely, the confusion consists of. Next, granting that he has been enlightened on these points, he may want to know why another rehash of the main events of the subject should help to correct the situation.

The best way to learn why previous writings about Roosevelt have tended not to diminish but to add to the confusion on the subject is to examine the writings. It would take too long to study them all, nor is this necessary, since most of the writings are not only opinionated but also, quite properly, concerned more with specific actions than with the personal causes that lie behind the actions. To concentrate on efforts to get at the nature of the man himself simplifies the job considerably, but there is still a good-sized box of books left to be considered. These can be divided into two shelves: those whose authors were pro- and those whose authors were anti-Roosevelt.

Of the pro-Roosevelt books, leaving out those by the President himself, since these are unrewarding, the best is definitely *My Boy Franklin* written by his mother, with the aid of Isabel Leighton and Gabrielle Forbush, in

1933. The book is good because it is a mine of neat, character-revealing detail and anecdote, and because one feels instinctively that it is mostly true. Mrs. Roosevelt obviously had access to better material than any of the President's other biographers. Her work goes far to substantiate the plausible theory that good writing is primarily a matter of having something to say; and her ghost writers appear to have fulfilled their function properly by remaining, so far as the effect upon the reader is concerned, invisible. Nonetheless, Mrs. Roosevelt had inevitably a strongly partisan attitude toward her subject; and while this may have helped her greatly in her work— whether or not a biographer hates his subject he must be able to sympathize with him—it limits the book's value as a rounded appraisal, which it does not purport to be.

Roosevelt's official biographer, so far as he has one, appears to be Mr. Ernest Lindley, an able Washington correspondent who has known the President since 1928. Lindley has written three books and innumerable stories about the President. His books are absolutely first-rate from the point of view of craftsmanship but one leaves them with the feeling that Mr. Lindley is really more interested in presenting a case than in presenting a personality and therefore that, judging the work on its intention, the test is not how much one now knows about the President but whether or not one would choose to vote for him. Lindley also often avails himself of the biographer's equivalent of poetic license, whereby he credits the hero with having motivated actions taken in name. This is a convenient device. It tends to give body and importance to a story and, perhaps for that reason, has been traditionally regarded as permissible or even essential. Nonetheless, it is a risky one, from the point of view of clarity.

After Mrs. Roosevelt and Lindley, the quality of the pro-Roosevelt volumes drops. There is one well-known name among their authors, that of Emil Ludwig. Ludwig's book seems only too clearly to have been a labor of love, but of cupboard love. There is a rancid taste about the rich servings of pseudo-psychiatric poetry and fervent speculation which he ladles out with the meretricious enthusiasm of a headwaiter palming off a dish of yesterday's pastry. If one wants mere admiration, Mrs. Roosevelt's work is preferable. Most of the rest of the pro-Roosevelt books are vapid collections of anecdote, like a little volume got out by a Boston preacher called *These Amazing Roosevelts*, or dreary campaign biographies, which, through the patent poor judgment of the authors, really belittle the subject they intend to praise.

Anti-Roosevelt literature is by definition subject to most of the same flaws as the campaign biographies. The only really notable item on the list is John Flynn's bitter little volume called *Country Squire in the White House*. Mr. Flynn's book is composed with a hearty venom that makes it highly readable. Unfortunately, his theme, which would have served for a brilliant chapter, is too slight to sustain an entire volume and in the effort to make it do so the author breaks it down entirely. The reader realizes that to criticize Roosevelt for being a country squire in the White House is like criticizing Lincoln for having been an Illinois lawyer, or Washington for having been a Virginia gentleman, in the White House. Certainly, presidents come from many walks of life; but that is their virtue, not their fault. All that is relevant is whether or not the Virginia gentleman, or the Illinois lawyer, or the country squire makes a good president. And by showing that Roosevelt does maintain a residence at Hyde Park, Mr. Flynn by no means proves that on this account he should not have another one on Pennsylvania Avenue.

Three other books on the Roosevelt shelf
have a special corner to themselves. These are
*Roosevelt and His America,* by Bernard Fay,
*The Roosevelt Family in America,* by Bellamy
Partridge, and *Roosevelt: Dictator or Democrat,* by Gerald W. Johnson. Fay, at present
in Paris where he has been accused of fascist
leanings, takes a generous view of the President and makes many naïve but trenchant
observations about Roosevelt's effect on the
country, not the least valid of which is the
implication in the third word of his title.
Partridge weaves together with relish and
dexterity the biographies of the clan's two
most recent contributions. Gerald Johnson
weighs the arguments about issues connected
with the President and assures the reader that
most of the arguments have a false relation
to the person to whom the issues relate. He
assumes, however, that, along with other
eminent men, Roosevelt has a public and a
private character and that the biographer
should therefore concern himself chiefly with
the public character, since this affects the
lives of millions, whereas the private character is really important only to the few people around him.

If, after reading a dozen or two books about
President Roosevelt, one comes to the con-

clusion that the net effect is far from con-
clusive one can go back to the source material
from which these were chiefly derived: the
files of newspapers and magazines covering
the period of his activity in public life. This
is a formidable task. The envelopes on Roosevelt in the Time, Inc. morgue, for example,
number five hundred. Each contains as many
words as the average volume. As a subject for
professional commentators, Mr. Roosevelt began his career with a bang when he was
elected to the New York State Senate in 1910.
At that time a reporter named W. A. Warn,
attracted by the similarity of the name to
Theodore Roosevelt's, wrote the first full-
length biographical sketch of Franklin, which
appeared in the New York *Times* for January
22, 1911. A trickle of Roosevelt material ran
through the papers of the next decade. The
newspaper morgues are fat for the year 1920,
when he ran for vice-president, and for the
years 1928 to 1932, when he was governor of
New York.

Since 1932, Roosevelt has been, in all prob-
ability, the most widely written-about man in
the world, and by now, more has been written
and said about him than about any other man
in history during his lifetime. It is a sad commentary on the much-heralded values of a free

press, radio, and movie industry if, at this late date, we do not know all there is to know about him. However, if we do know all about him, it is an even sadder commentary on the value of knowledge that we cannot reach a conclusion on the subject; and this brings us to the business of defining the confusion about Mr. Roosevelt which should be understood as to cause, kind and degree.

Since Roosevelt is, increasingly, a world figure, it will be as well to assess the confusion about him on a world scale. Here we have at once a new element to consider. While it is precisely the improvement in communications, physical and verbal, that makes international understanding in general and international understanding of Roosevelt in particular so essential, it is also the inevitable time lag in communications that increases the difficulty of such understanding. To make this case as clear as possible, we may take the case of His Majesty Abdul Aziz Ibn Saud, King of Saudi Arabia, who, in a shrinking world, is one of the many heads of state whose personal stake in knowing more about Mr. Roosevelt is comparatively recent. For his Majesty, however, this task—which is complex enough for a citizen of the United States—is additionally complicated by the fact that he has no conception whatever of what the United States is like, nor can he hope to get one. Sitting comfortably in the throne room of his remote palace of Riyadh, surrounded by several thousand square miles of desert underlaid with oil, Ibn Saud is not only unaware of the nature of the present United States president. He is also unaware of the nature of presidents in general, and indeed of practically everything else of which United States everyday life is composed, from Tootsie Rolls to turbines. However, it would be erroneous to suppose that Ibn Saud, because he has no true picture of America, is without a mental picture of Roosevelt. Just as a United States citizen who may chance to have heard of Ibn Saud pictures him in terms of his own experience, including fiction, that is, as a kind of composite of Rudolph Valentino, Lawrence of Arabia and King Solomon, just so this remote monarch pictures Roosevelt in terms of his experience, which does not include fiction reading. The King is no doubt aware that Roosevelt wears pants instead of a *mishla*, but it would be hard for him to envisage a ruler who could not have people's heads cut off or whose wife writes a newspaper column. Indeed, the very fact that, while Ibn Saud has seen a hundred or so wives, he has never

seen any newspaper column at all is just
the kind of international confusion about
Roosevelt—compounded a thousand times
with regard to other heads of state, who in
addition to not being able to envisage or
understand Mr. Roosevelt clearly are also
unable to envisage or understand each other
—that complicates international relations
and makes for recurring wars.

Ibn Saud is, of course, an extreme and isolated, though by no means a unique, case. To
get at a more common, and thus more important one, let us consider the confusion about
Mr. Roosevelt that exists in England. Saudi
Arabia is considerably and increasingly concerned with the United States President, as is
every other corner of the globe, but England
is intimately concerned with him, and that
for much less subterranean reasons. The English are a diligent and industrious race;
Roosevelt is a household name in England,
just as Churchill is in the United States, and
there are many points in common about the
standing of these two leaders vis-à-vis the
populations of each other's countries.

To an American in England it may often
seem astounding that some of the cloudy
grandeur that attaches to the noble figure of
Churchill when seen from a distance vanishes

on closer acquaintance. The British, while they admire "Winnie," are inclined to think of him less as a hero than as a prime minister subject to re-election or not, as they may see fit. On the question of Roosevelt, the British take a different view. To an Englishman Roosevelt seems an altogether satisfactory figure primarily on account of what they think are his views on the war. Quite over and above this, however, is the fact that he seems satisfactory on other grounds. English people naturally, and correctly, regard Americans as crude and uproarious as compared to themselves. They therefore find in Roosevelt reassuring evidence that Americans may have some sense of the fitness of things after all.

Roosevelt is just the sort of man who might have been a great success in British public life —a member of the ruling class, entitled to an old school tie, and at the same time patently motivated by a strong sense of cricket. That Roosevelt also speaks the English language with both phonetic and grammatical accuracy—an accomplishment as general in England as it is exceptional in the United States —appears to be the final hallmark. Englishmen as a rule are delighted to discuss Roosevelt with Americans, because the subject seems to be inviting. But if the American

takes an anti-Roosevelt slant, the Englishman
will in most cases assume that the American is
either a purblind isolationist, a disappointed
rentier or a guttersnipe, and ungrateful to
Providence into the bargain. He will, however, politely attempt to conceal this unflatter-
ing opinion, which is more usually than can
be said for the American when he has heard
his ally's views on Mr. Churchill.

That the views of the Eastern potentates
and of the Englishman in the street on the
subject of Mr. Roosevelt should be divergent
both with each other and also with the truth
is perhaps natural enough. It would be contradictory indeed if human perceptions surpassed that degree rendered desirable by the
developments attained through previous
human perceptions; or, in other words, if
information rendered essential by the air
age were available before the air age started.
However, getting closer to home, we might
conceivably expect that the American grasp
of the problem would be clearer.

What we find, on the contrary, is that, while
the general area of disagreement about Roosevelt is smaller—no American really mistakes
him either for an emir or an Old Etonian—
the intensity of the disagreement is, by this
very compression, vastly increased. Nor is this

surprising. The fact is that the recent vast increase of communications has made it possible for everyone to find out what everyone else thinks at the time when he thinks it. For better of for worse, in a land of complete communicational development, free opinion, and lively articulation, this means that the quantity of opinion about Mr. Roosevelt, through newspapers, the radio and common cracker-barrel gossip has long since surpassed the ability of any individual human mind to absorb it. Most people either just made up their minds on the matter long ago, and stopped trying, or else they change their minds on the basis of day-to-day events because they have long since realized the impracticality of getting to the heart of the matter.

What the exact extremes of opinion about Roosevelt may be, who may hold them, and how far they may be in the process of changing need not concern us. But the real nature of Mr. Roosevelt does concern us, and what America knows about the real nature of Mr. Roosevelt appears so far to have been best expressed by Mark Sullivan. Summarizing all the considered judgments of his contemporaries, Sullivan came to the conclusion that Roosevelt was an enigma and that no satisfactory portrait of him has been or can be written.

That Roosevelt is an enigma seems to be a fairly well-founded impression; although it certainly contradicts the assumption of the present author, who announced a few pages back that human character as a whole, not Roosevelt's only, is entirely simple and as easy to solve as the problem of two times two. So far, however, this author in his efforts to solve the problem has used up 167 pages. In the course of these pages he has called the President a seal, a whippersnapper, David, St. George, the captain of what seems to be no more than that ancient tug, the Ship of State, an oral personality, a shark, an Arabian emir, and a good many other things. He has used adjectives from devious to courageous, and he has had the President doing everything from exhibiting myopia to firing metaphysical pellets through an electrical device. Unless, in the course of all this, a solution to the riddle has been at least approached, it would seem to argue either that Roosevelt is an enigma or else that the author is incompetent as well as boastful, which would be a most unwelcome premise.

Before attempting to clear up the Roosevelt enigma for good and all, there is one fairly general misconception about the Presidency itself which requires correction. This is the idea that a president is a man who (a) sees what needs to be done to the country, (b) works out a scheme for doing it, and (c) tries to get elected so that he can put his scheme into effect. It is easy enough to see how this conception arises. At the party conventions a platform, or scheme, is drawn up, and the candidate then campaigns on the basis that he will try to put this scheme into effect. Nonetheless, the conception is illusory because there lies behind it an antecedent set of circumstances which, though usually overlooked, are more fundamental. In fact, the President is, or should be, simply a man whose character and previous experience have given him justified confidence in his ability to deal with any situation that may come up, no matter how big or taxing. It is this general conviction that not only usually does, but should, underlie his efforts to get elected; and the actual program that he sets up is, and probably should be, a mere afterthought, an addenda, one of innumerable other programs which he has developed or can develop as circumstances require. In even more general terms, people whose primary concern is not with action but with thoughts are very necessary people, but they rarely come to positions of active power; and when they do, they usually mishandle these positions.

In addition to a general confidence in his ability to handle anything that may come up, a president needs, of course, some sort of well-tested and reasonable frame of reference to guide him in doing so. This is not to be confused with a completely indexed personal constitution, neatly ticketed and filed, much less with a specific program. It may be, and in the case of a few articulate presidents has been, a fairly well-defined philosophy of life in general and of government in particular; or it may just be a general feeling of sympathy for the underdog, enthusiasm for law and order, or what not. When the president gets into office, he soon discovers that his original program as outlined by the party platform is subject to alteration by influences ranging all the way from Congress to the weather. If he had nothing but the program to go by he would be in poor state from the outset. What he really has to do in most cases is just throw away the music and begin to play by ear. The audience is naturally extremely curious to find out what the tune is.

In Roosevelt's case there is no doubt whatever that, by the time he set out to run for president, he had acquired a sense of assurance which, justified or otherwise, made him feel equal to any situation. Granted an assured capacity for improvisation, however, the next question is what kind of frame of reference be used. Roosevelt's can be summarized fairly readily. The President, like most other little boys who are closer to their mothers than to their fathers, grew up with a certain liking for, and identification with, the weaker elements in society. This tendency, easily defined as simply sympathy, he shares with perhaps half the rest of the human race and with such divergent types of leaders as Leon Trotsky, Abraham Lincoln and Marcus Aurelius, so that, in itself, it is not especially revealing. In the President's case, however, it is associated with a lack of sympathy for, or at least interest in, fatherly and dominating types of people. This trait the President has always exhibited both positively, in his choice of associates, and negatively, in the people he has opposed. If we cease to investigate the President's frame of reference at this point, it is not to say that he has no political philosophy, but only that this is the emotional foundation on which the philosophy must be based, and of which the philosophy will, therefore, be the rationale.

Given the general picture of the President's

function, and the mainspring of his political responses, the next point to examine is his method. As to this, the President himself has never made  any secret of it. He functions by means of people. To some degree this is true of all executives and especially of all presidents. Even presidents, however, have their choice of several other methods: one is to go to books; another is to take solitary thought; a third might be to seek a precedent. Roosevelt is not much of a reader, he dislikes solitude, and he scarcely understands the nature of a precedent. On the contrary, other people, as fragments of the life which he finds so enthralling or even perhaps as imitations of himself, have always enchanted him; and to say that he uses them as tutors is only a partial statement of the fact that he also uses them in every other capacity as constantly as possible.

It would be preposterous to suppose, for example, that the New Deal—which Roosevelt calmly brushed off in the winter of 1943 as though it had been something someone else thought up—was a kind of Hitlerian New Order which Roosevelt laboriously dreamed up as an improvement for the American way of life and which he then set himself to put into effect. Rather, Roosevelt came to the conclusion, inevitable in view of his situation and his character, that he not only wanted to be, but ought to be, president. Only after reaching this decision did he begin seriously to consider what to do when he reached Washington. Once having addressed himself to this second question, he proceeded characteristically. He surrounded himself with a crew of people, none of whom, with the exception of Hugh Johnson, were nearly as old or anything like as powerful as he was. The result was a fine set of plans most of which, by the time he got to the White House, were outdated and impractical and the rest of which he discarded subsequently. As soon as he became president, Roosevelt encountered a first-rate crisis, which stimulated him to an unparalleled frenzy of healthy enjoyment and activity which, though unplanned, was effective. Not content with the Cabinet officers and Congress, who are more than plenty of people for most presidents, he immediately began to acquire new ones, popping them into various new organizations of all sorts which seemed to be modeled, if on anything at all, on the potting sheds, stables and outbuildings of Hyde Park.

In recording events, writers, and especially newspaper writers, often use a convenient shorthand in which men's names stand for the actions which they initiate or influence. But it would be misreading this shorthand to suppose that the actions are necessarily motivated by a desire to attain precisely the results that attend them; and, owing to Roosevelt's peculiarly informal and haphazard technique, the distortion involved in such misreading would be peculiarly acute in his case. Having observed how Roosevelt really operates, it is permissible to conclude that, while the New Deal bears a discernible relation to his character, it is no more an accurate outline of it than a shadow at sunset is an accurate silhouette. A good part of the confusion about Roosevelt comes from a failure to make allowance for this distinction between what Roosevelt is and what has happened more or less indirectly because of him. Furthermore, since the projection of Roosevelt in the events of our time is an immeasurably larger configuration than Roosevelt himself, and since the confusion about Roosevelt is in proportion to the projection rather than the person, it is not especially surprising that the confusion should have reached considerable dimensions.

As to the motivations of Roosevelt himself, the original and most basic motivation is quite simply attention, using this word in its broadest sense. This is not a damaging diagnosis; for the love of attention, using this word in its present connotation, is neither a frivolous nor an exceptional affinity. Attention, usually parental attention, is a prerequisite to survival for every human being. The later demands which human beings make upon life—for power, wealth, prestige or what not—may be construed as extensions or replicas of this original, well-founded need, and may be defined in terms of it. Power, for instance, is in itself perhaps an abstraction. The exciting thing about power, what makes it desirable, is that everyone pays, or can be obliged to pay, attention to the person who has it. Money has been defined by such authorities as Thorstein Veblen as a mechanism used chiefly and fundamentally for securing attention. Prestige, of course, is by definition merely attention in an especially tasty form. That few people will readily confess to an appetite for attention is proof neither that the appetite is vicious nor that they do not entertain it. When anyone tries to define what he wants from life, this invariably comes down to something which can easily be regarded as a form of attention, usually a wholesome form; furthermore, it can invariably be shown to be a derivative of the wholesome attention he received as an infant.

Of course, where Roosevelt is concerned, the process is especially clear. Like most other infants, he began by requiring and securing the attention of his mother, first by means of yowling and then, by a conventional improvement, through the use of words. Soon he broadened his range and got other people's attention in the same way. The only remarkable thing about Roosevelt's case was that nothing occurred to thwart this healthy process or to cramp it into special and less profitable channels. Whereas most people are obliged by circumstances to seek attention either in counterfeit forms, like money, or on a limited scale, like mere domesticity, no such disadvantageous limitations operated against Roosevelt. Instead, owing to his healthy psyche and to the conditions of his home life, his education and his career in politics, his ambitions in this direction retained their original purity while changing only in regard to size. Disdaining the feeble imitations with which most human beings must perforce satisfy themselves, he demanded attention only in its finest, essential form. His ability to satisfy his demands, increased by many years of practice, which also increased the demands themselves through force of habit, was finally equipped with a sort of extra supercharger, when he suffered his paralysis.

The main question about the desire for attention is not whether people have it but how they gratify it. Thus, to secure God's attention, by saintly doings, or one's family's attention, by supporting them, is a socially acceptable and praiseworthy method. To attain notoriety, by standing on one's head at the opera, or the attention of the police force and the newspapers, by committing robberies, is a less admirable scheme. In Roosevelt's case, opinion as to the validity of his methods will most often depend chiefly on whether or not the opinion-holder himself has gained or lost attention or a substitute therefor through the actions for which he holds the President accountable. Where the President himself is concerned it is clear at least that the attention he sought was from appropriate sources; that he sought it according to approved usage; and, finally, that he sought it with unprecedented efficacy.

Since the search for approbation—to use a less obnoxious, though also less exact term —is universal, to disparage such an effort would be belittling human life in general; and it is precisely because the search for approbation is practically synonymous with life itself that Roosevelt's chief preoccupation can be so simply diagnosed. Roosevelt's enthusiasm for crisis is simply a manifestation of his enthusiasm for life itself because a crisis represents life in its most lively form. The highest form of human attention is also properly reserved especially for those who can deal with crises successfully, and the quantity so reserved is in marked contrast with the quantity that goes to those who can deal only with humdrum matters. Likewise, Roosevelt's devotion to people is wholehearted, because people are good attentive beings. The only element lacking in his whole happy adjustment seems to be a sense of conservation or restraint entirely proportionate to his enthusiasm for existence as defined above. This failing must be noted as the obverse of his virtues, since it clearly derives from precisely that blissful unsophistication about the effects of authority which permitted his ego to escape the impeding effects of punishment for overexpansion and punishment's resultant fear.

So far as any enigma about Roosevelt is concerned, the chief enigma seems to be why, in attempting to understand someone whose basic motivations have always been so crystal-clear and so effectively expressed, anyone should ever have failed in the attempt. The most plausible answer to this more tantalizing riddle seems to lie in precisely that sense of guilt of which the President is so totally free. Perhaps it is chiefly because their greed for attention is so extensive or their capacity to gratify it so feeble that most persons shudder at the thought of possessing such an appetite at all. Naturally, if people are shocked by the thought that they themselves are animated by the wish to secure attention, they repress even more sternly the thought that they should be led by, and thus, in a sense, inferior to, someone in whom this wish is not only present but entirely unconcealed. And thus they end up by misunderstanding not only Franklin Roosevelt's character but, even less excusably, their own.

Much has been said about Roosevelt's attitude toward posterity. Certain of his actions, such as preparing his state papers year by year or setting up a museum of Rooseveltiana at Hyde Park, or helping Professor Samuel Morison to write the history of the war, have led many commentators to suppose that he has an overly developed "sense of history." It has been proposed that the President not only dramatizes himself in regard to his contemporaries, as all men do, but also dramatizes himself for the audience of the future, as though acting simultaneously for both a studio and an unseen audience.

This theory may contain considerable truth. It would be remarkable if any man whose career assured him of a role in history, let alone a man with Roosevelt's well-developed sense of drama, should be insensible to how the role is to be written. On the other hand, it seems probable that no one with Roosevelt's relish of immediate contemporary attention should ever choose to forego his enjoyment of this in order to savor the mere bouquet of problematical attention from unborn generations. In other words, Roosevelt's quite permissible desire to cut a fine figure for the future must be outweighed in his own mind by his even stronger desire to cut a fine figure for the present.

However this may be, even if Roosevelt did have a clear idea of the role he wants to occupy in history, and the foolish inclination to devote much of his time to creating that role, it would do him little good. The view that history takes of people rarely corresponds with the view they might want it to take. Contrary to happy superstition, it does not even necessarily take a true view, unless we are content to define all thought as wishful and truth merely as that which we believe. For example, if the Germans had won the war and thus come to dominate the world, German theories about the past would doubtless have dominated the history of the future. Hitler would have been assayed as a superman, and Roosevelt as a knave. As things stand, the reverse will probably occur; but to suppose that such a happy outcome is always attained would be to suppose that right makes might, which is a most debatable theorem. Before we can know what role Roosevelt will play in the histories of the future we would have to know from what point of view the histories will be written; and it would be a rash man indeed who would attempt to predict this from present indications. The present is merely the theater of war in which the forces of the future contend for mastery. And by definition no contestant in this struggle can hope also to be a spectator of it. All that can be done at present in appraising Roosevelt's position in history is to examine the facts which the historians will have to draw upon; and to consider the extremes of interpretation to which these facts are susceptible.

If history were to place a favorable interpretation on the facts of Franklin Roosevelt's career, it is not hard to see how he might come to occupy, in the Muzzeys of the coming centuries, a position analogous to that once occupied by George Washington, albeit on a higher plane. Let us assume that, after a wise peace has been written, and after a successful period of moral and industrial reconversion, the world in general and the United States in particular enters a period of universal prosperity. The national debt is reduced, Stalin becomes a good democrat, and the Imperial House of Japan devotes its influence to encouraging the art of fan painting. Under those conditions it would by no means be unthinkable that Roosevelt should be regarded as a wise, fatherly and farseeing executive in whose beautifully proportioned career the brilliant setting in order of his own nation was merely a prelude to the brave and even more brilliant reformation of civilization as a whole. The great man's squabbles with the backward judges of the Supreme Court, his sweeping plans for the reformation of big business and agriculture, his heroic ventures into world planning, sketched out in broad outline during the midst of the world's last war, could become the raw material for a new age of epic poetry. Meanwhile satirists would amuse themselves by prying into old newspaper files for material on the absurd diatribes of the Roosevelt haters, which would seem analogous to the anti-Lincoln cartoons in the newspaper files of the 1860's.

Of course, the opposite may come to pass. Perhaps the peace will not be a just one. Stalin or his successor may fail to sympathize with the Atlantic Charter. Instead of entering the millennium, or anything even approximating it, we may enter an era when taxes rise, wars continue, and the American way of life changes, beyond recognition, for the worse. Surely in such case historians will find Franklin Roosevelt partly to blame. If civil commotion develops, he will be faulted for having set class against class; if fascism impends, it will be recalled that he was its mild forerunner. Roosevelt's readiness to run for a third term, if not a fourth, will be the point on which the argument turns. Far from a wise and justifiable break with outworn custom, this will seem an ultimate betrayal of public trust. Reflective writers will show that, just because the American system was such a flexible one, those unwritten traditions which were implicit in it were all the more precious because of their rarity, and that the two-term tradition was especially precious beyond all the rest. While a parvenu might have been forgiven for failing to respect such a tradition, such writers could contend that for an American of Roosevelt's background and upbringing to do so was a gross, humiliating and disastrous breach of propriety and manners.

In fact, of course, neither of these two extremes is likely to govern the idiom of the unborn historian. What is more likely to occur is that the world will rock along from good to bad much as it always has done in the past and that Roosevelt's biographers will be compelled to choose a middle course of some sort, weighted favorably or otherwise as the outcome of events suggests.

For those handicapped by their temporal proximity to the subject, all that can be said about Roosevelt in the way of judgment is irrelevant, except in so far as it may affect the part he is allowed to play in the battle that will determine his eventual valuation. On the whole, then, using common words in their ordinary senses, it appears that he is a good but not a very wise man; vain, captious, overconfident, and warmhearted; no more honest than most, but friendlier than the average; courageous but at the same time, all things considered, so far as human beings can be capable of such a thing, not totally without a certain somewhat meretricious grandeur.

Roosevelt has, after all, maintained control of events to some degree, through the most trying period of United States history to date. Although partially responsible for getting us into a two-front war, he seems even more responsible for the likelihood that we will emerge from it better off than before, and into a better world.

The question of shaping a world involves the question of what shape one wants to give it, and what influence Roosevelt has had in this respect. Most "great men" of the past have been men whose ideas were firmly settled, whose actions followed a discernible central thesis, who had an idea they wanted to impose; whereas, Roosevelt, if he has one, has successfully concealed it.

One could say that, whereas great men in the conventional pattern are not content with striving against authority but wish to replace previous authority with a plan of their own, Roosevelt's aim is merely the contest; and that, given the chance to attain a settled outcome, he throws it away and allows a new set of contentions to arise. Thus, just as the victory in his first term was inherently bound to end up in the commotion of the second, his Atlantic Charter seems bound to wind up in the commotion of the whole world; indeed, this document may have been subconsciously designed to perpetuate the only crisis of which control is really out of his reach.

This leads to a consideration of whether such a state of affairs is for the worse or for the better. Possibly it is in the wood of the American system to produce not tidy planners, whose regimes would be seriously subject to demolishment by their successors in any case, but rather brilliant improvisers and extemporaneous magicians. And possibly just the qualities of brilliance in crisis and enjoyment of struggle for its own sake that make such men acceptable to Americans, are what prevents them from attaining the formalized results of great men in the historic European sense. And possibly, boiled down to its ultimate essence, this is not a wholly disadvantageous arrangement.

Just as we make it easy for such people to get control of the country we also make it easy for ourselves to get rid of them; and the result is that by and large we never come to expect too much of them. In a tyranny, old style or new, the reverse process is effected; the head of state is by definition the executive type and invites judgment on the grounds of his efficiency. It goes without saying that if he is inefficient he loses his job; but what is less generally appreciated is that even if he is efficient he also loses his job eventually, through death or overextension. And this leaves an enormous gap which there is no way of filling except by the discovery of a new dictator. It is this general defect that makes it so hard to set up "democracy" in nations which have never been used to it; and it is in the avoidance of such catastrophic ups-and-downs that democracy, which appears to reward human mediocrity but in fact merely recognizes human imperfection, really serves its purpose. Under these conditions, continuing commotion is an asset, not a liability; and Roosevelt deserves thanks for achieving it.

Certainly, if nations traded leaders the way baseball clubs trade pitchers, there are few Americans who would want to swap Roosevelt for any of the spitball artists on the other clubs. We have the feeling that he is a product of a much better farm system; and rated against the international field, according to the American standard, his average is easily the best available. Of course, this is not to say the same thing about Roosevelt as compared to other Americans. The essence of his virtues—including precisely the fact that he likes commotion so much that he never does much about getting things properly straightened out—is precisely that they are by no means unique, any more than his defects. And the woods are full of other Americans who possess both in greater or less degree. It is only necessary to discover them.

Meanwhile, all things considered, whether we have him with us much longer or not, Franklin Roosevelt still seems to be on his game, if not quite at the top of it in the fateful summer months of 1944. The subtle toxins of authority may have impaired his competence to some degree but even in this respect he has an advantage of sorts. At least his psychic system has had time to adjust itself to such poisons and there is thus no likelihood that any alarming new symptoms of self-infatuation will set in, as might well be the case with some of his competitors.

Polite and assured, full of seasoned stamina and lively as a cricket, he seems still quite ready to enjoy a series of new and even more exciting crises. Sitting with a caller in his upstairs study he sometimes pushes his free-wheeling chair back from his cluttered desk and sits still for a minute chewing reflectively on the tip of his cigarette holder. At such moments the deep lines in Roosevelt's face suggest that he is listening to some sound that pleases him—as though the subdued hum of the household behind the closed door, the murmur of the capital beyond the curtained windows, and further away still the vast chatter of the continents all blended together for him into a sort of music in whose warm and complex counterpoint he found comfort and a sense of ultimate harmony.

*Set in Linotype Baskerville*
*Format by A. W. Rushmore*
*Manufactured by the Haddon Craftsmen*
*Published by* HARPER & BROTHERS
*New York and London*